Praise for
First Scientist: Ibn al-Haytham

"Bradley Steffens's engaging style makes the life and works of one of the greatest scholars in history accessible to the modern audience. It is an excellent introduction to not only a great mind in human history whose discoveries a millennium ago continue to benefit us in the modern world but also the larger field of history of Islamic mathematics and science. Unfortunately, due to the dominance of a Eurocentric narrative of science globally, the contributions to mathematics and sciences from the medieval Islamic civilization are largely ignored and underappreciated. The story of the great scholar Ibn al-Haytham is a striking example of this larger phenomenon. The fascinating story of a remarkable polymath in this captivating book will make you finish it in one sitting and want to keep it nearby for easy reference. Along the way, you will also learn about the Islamic culture and the larger context and issues. *First Scientist: Ibn al-Haytham* fills a significant void in the literature and the new, updated version is even more attractive and engaging than the original edition. It will be highly appreciated by anyone who is interested in the history of science."
—Nuh Aydin, Professor of Mathematics, Kenyon College

"This new coffee table edition of Steffens's biography of Ibn al-Haytham is a thing of beauty, with stunning photographs and illustrations adding to the scholarly yet accessible biographical text. Ibn al-Haytham is rightly regarded as one of the greatest scientists in history and should be a household name everywhere in the world. The fact that he led such a colourful life is a delightful bonus. I will be recommending this book to everyone I know, and even those I don't."
—Jim Al-Khalili, author of *The House of Wisdom: How Arabic Science Saved Ancient Knowledge and Gave Us the Renaissance*

"Ever wondered how we see? Ever wondered how they found out what really happens and how? Anyone interested in the history of science, optics, maths, the scientific method and how it all began should read this fascinating book. It is revelatory, riveting and quite revolutionary. It could change the way you see the world."
—Brigitte Nerlich, Emeritus Professor of Science, Language and Society, University of Nottingham

"This book is a must read for anyone who wishes to learn about a forgotten chapter in history, enjoys the true spirit of inquiry, and is an eternal seeker of truth. Steffens has a unique ability of a storyteller that makes the reading of his book as interesting as a spy thriller, unfolding the events in Ibn al-Haytham's life like the clues being discovered by a forensic detective."
—Husain F. Nagamia, MD, *Journal of the Islamic Medical Association of North America*

"In this clearly written, carefully reasoned profile, Steffens not only traces the scantly documented life of one of early modern science's giants, but also places him both within the broader contexts of early Muslim society, and of the whole history of science. The many color pictures enhance this illuminating narrative with maps, diagrams, and images of illustrated manuscript pages."
—*Kirkus Reviews*

"Steffens has written a wonderfully clear and concise account of Ibn al-Haytham's life and work. The quality of the book is excellent. It is wonderfully typeset and contains many full-color illustrations that bring the era and the science to life."
—*Skulls in the Stars*

"I congratulate Bradley Steffens for his beautiful work about Ibn al-Haytham and his advancement of experimental science. Steffens goes into great detail about how Ibn al-Haytham performed his research to arrive at his conclusions. Because Ibn al-Haytham established and used the scientific method as we know it today, it becomes apparent why the author calls him the first scientist."
—Ertan Salik, Professor of Physics at Cal Poly University, *The Fountain*

"Like the history of mathematics, the history of science is incomplete without an acknowledgment of early scholars in the Middle East. This clearly written introduction to Ibn al-Haytham, his society, and his contributions does that."
—Carolyn Phelan, *Booklist*

"Steffens deftly weaves an overview of Muslim history into this biography. No one can dispute Ibn al-Haytham's unique contributions to science in both Islam and western culture. Numerous illustrations from Arab and European sources enhance the text. This book would make an excellent supplement to units about world history and the history of science."
—Pat Sherman, reviewer

First
Scientist

IBN AL-HAYTHAM

First
Scientist

IBN AL-HAYTHAM

Bradley Steffens

BLUE DOME

Published by Blue Dome Press
335 Clifton Ave.
Clifton, NJ, 07011, USA
www.bluedomepress.com

Library of Congress Cataloging-in-Publication Data

Names: Steffens, Bradley, 1955- author.
Title: First Scientist : Ibn al-Haytham / Bradley Steffens.
Description: Clifton, NJ : Blue Dome Press, [2020] | Includes
    bibliographical references and index.
Identifiers: LCCN 2020045547 (print) | LCCN 2020045548 (ebook) | ISBN
    9781682060292 (paperback) | ISBN 9781682065341 (ebook)
Subjects: LCSH: Alhazen, 965-1039. | Muslim scientists--Iraq--Biography. |
    Scientists--Iraq--Biography. | Science--Middle East--History--To 1500. |
    Islam and science--History--To 1500. | Islamic Empire--Intellectual
    life.
Classification: LCC Q143.A46 S74 2020 (print) | LCC Q143.A46 (ebook) |
    DDC 509.2 [B]--dc23
LC record available at https://lccn.loc.gov/2020045547
LC ebook record available at https://lccn.loc.gov/2020045548

Paperback 978-1-68206-029-2
Ebook 978-1-68206-534-1

CONTENTS

PREFACE

This is the first full biography of the eleventh-century Islamic scholar Al-Hasan ibn al-Haytham to be published in the West. The book attempts to bring to light the life, contributions, and impact of one of the most fascinating, but equally unnoticed, figures of scientific history, in the context of a broad overview of his era and a brief history of the spread of Islam. Prior to the publication of the first edition of this book in 2007, Ibn al-Haytham was known in the West, if at all, for introducing algebra into geometrical proofs and for taking the first steps towards the development of the branch of mathematics known as analytic geometry. Some Western scholars also knew him as the first person to accurately describe the physics behind the projection of images through apertures—the process that underlies the workings of the human eye, the camera obscura, film cameras, and even digital cameras. Those are important contributions to mathematics and science, but as I read his massive treatise on light and vision, *Kitāb al-Manāzir* or *Book of Optics*, while researching this book I was struck by something even more significant; namely, that he systematically used experiments, which he called "true demonstrations," to test his hypotheses about the propagation of light.

Whether by using a straight copper tube to test whether light rays traveled in straight lines or by employing an aperture in a copper sheet to determine whether light rays from different sources interfered with one another as they passed through the opening, Ibn al-Haytham was practicing experimental science some six hundred years before Galileo Galilei, four hundred years before Leonardo da Vinci, and two hundred years before Roger Bacon, each of whom has been called "the first modern scientist" by various historians.

Not only did Ibn al-Haytham practice experimental science, he also understood its implications. He realized that the work of scholars—including himself—who supported their theories about natural phenomena with logic alone was fatally flawed. "We formerly composed a treatise on optics in which we often followed persuasive methods of reasoning," Ibn al-Haytham wrote in the introduction of *Kitāb al-Manāzir*, "but when true demonstrations relating to all objects of vision occurred to us, we started afresh the composition of this book. Whoever, therefore, comes upon the said treatise must know that it should be discarded." Thus, we can pinpoint the advent of experimental science not just to the lifetime of Ibn al-Haytham but to the precise moment, one thousand years ago, when he realized that logic alone was no longer sufficient grounds for knowing the truth about the natural world. This realization changed the course of human history, giving humankind a new and effective way of establishing facts about the natural world—an approach known today as the scientific method.

BOYHOOD IN BASRA

At the beginning of *Kitāb al-Manāzir*, or *Book of Optics*, the medieval mathematician Ibn al-Haytham expresses skepticism about the ability of human beings to understand the complex workings of nature. "When inquiry concerns subtle matters, perplexity grows, views diverge, opinions vary, conclusions differ, and certainty becomes difficult to obtain,"[1] he wrote. One of the problems with discovering the truth about nature, Ibn al-Haytham realized, is that human beings have physical limitations that can affect their observations. "The premises are gleaned from the senses," he wrote, "and the senses, which are our tools, are not immune from error."[2] Haunted by doubts about human perception and reason, Ibn al-Haytham searched for new ways to establish the validity of observations, hypotheses, theories, and conclusions. Knowing that mathematical equations and geometric proofs did not vary from person to person, he used mathematics to describe natural phenomena whenever possible. He also devised simple, repeatable experiments to test hypotheses. By systematically applying these methods of inquiry to his research, Ibn al-Haytham launched a new era in the history of learning—the age of experimental science.

The man who revolutionized the science was born in 965 in Basra, in what was then the Abbasid Caliphate and is now the Republic of Iraq. His full name, Abū ʿAlī al-Hasan ibn al-Hasan ibn al-Haytham, reveals several things about him and his family. The name is Arabic, indicating that his ancestors came from the Arabian peninsula. His *ism*, or given name, is al-Hasan, meaning "the handsome." *Ibn* means "the son of," revealing that his father also was named al-Hasan. His grandfather's name was al-Haytham, meaning "the lion." Centuries later, when unknown European scholars translated *Kitāb al-Manāzir* into Latin, they shortened the author's name to al-Hasan, which they wrote as "Alhazen" or "Alhacen." Other Western scholars adopted the same practice when they translated other books by Ibn al-Haytham. The Latinized version of Ibn al-Haytham's name became so engrained in Western society that even

"The Califate in 750." From *The Historical Atlas* by William R. Shepherd, 1926. Courtesy of the University of Texas Libraries, The University of Texas at Austin.

Within one hundred years, the Arab Muslims controlled an empire stretched from the Indus River in the east to the Iberian Peninsula in the west.

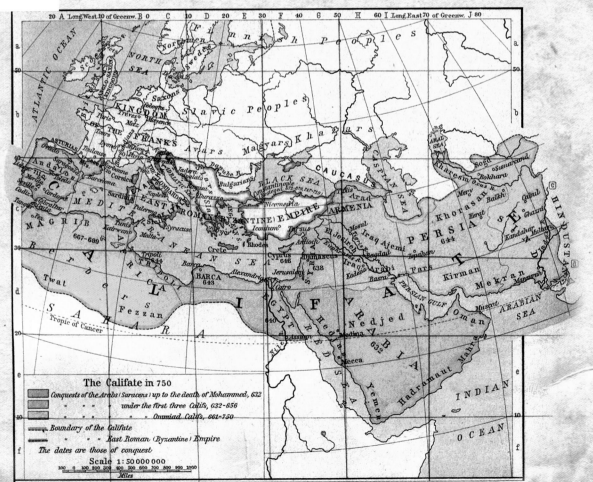

today most libraries—including the Library of Congress in Washington DC—list books by and about the Arab scientist under "Alhazen."

Ibn al-Haytham and his ancestors were adherents to the religion of Islam. The word "Islam" is an Arabic word that means "submission to the will of God." Accordingly, the followers of Islam are known as Muslims, or those who "submit" to God. Muslims worship one God, known in Arabic as Allah. Islam is one of three faiths, along with Judaism and Christianity, that traces its roots to a covenant between God and the ancient Chaldean patriarch Abraham. Muslims revere not only Abraham, but also some of the same prophets as Jews and Christians, including Moses, Noah, and Jesus. They believe that Muhammad ibn 'Abd Allah ibn 'Abd al-Muttalib, known as Prophet Muhammad, was the last of this long line of prophets, and Islam is the last religion until the Day of Judgment.

Arab Muslims swept out of the Arabian Peninsula around 630 and spread their faith to many neighboring lands. Within one hundred years, the Arab

> By systematically applying various methods of inquiry to his research, Ibn al-Haytham launched a new era in the history of learning— the age of experimental science.

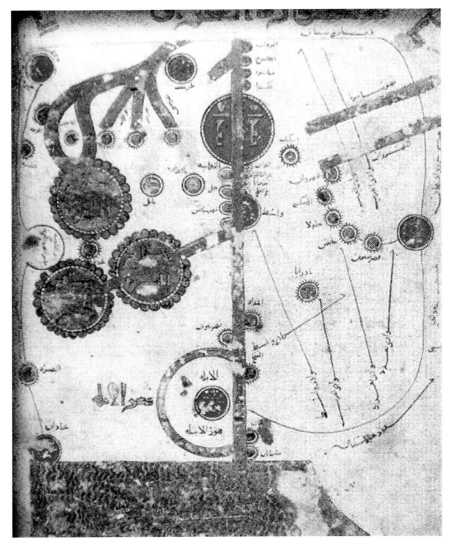

Al-Istakhri map of Tigris and Euphrates valley from Baghdad to Persian Gulf's coast (9th century). On ancient maps by Muslims, North is always found at the bottom of the page.

Muslims controlled an empire stretched from the Indus River in the east to the Iberian Peninsula in the west.

After settling the region between the Tigris and Euphrates Rivers, known as Mesopotamia, the Arab Muslims made the city of Mosul the seat of their new government. They also founded two new cities: Al-Kufah in the center of the country and Basra in the south. These outposts served as regional bases for Muslim rule. Waves of immigrants from Arabia settled in these new cities.

The Arab Muslims were eager to learn from the peoples they ruled. This thirst for knowledge sprang from the teachings of Islam, which exhorts the faithful to learn as much as possible about the universe. "Those who remember Allah [God]...reflect on the creation of the heavens and the earth."[3] declares the Qur'an, the holy book of the Muslims. Prophet Muhammad declared, "Seeking knowledge is a duty upon every Muslim."[4]

The Muslims were particularly interested in the writings of the ancient Greeks, who had lived along the northern coast of the Mediterranean Sea more than one thousand years earlier and had made important discoveries in the fields of philosophy, mathematics, medicine, and astronomy. Around 150 bce, the Greeks were conquered by the Romans, who ruled much of Europe, the Middle East and northern Africa for another 600 years. The Romans copied and spread ancient Greek writings—including books by philosophers such as Aristotle and Plato; mathematicians such as Archimedes, Euclid, and Apollonius of Perga; the physician Galen; and the astronomer Claudius Ptolemy—throughout their empire. Many wealthy Muslims paid scholars to translate the works of the ancient Greeks into Arabic.

One of the most active collectors of ancient Greek works was Abu Jafar al-Ma'mun ibn Harun, the caliph, or ruler, of the Abbasid Caliphate from 813 to 833. Determined to build one of the greatest libraries in the Islamic world, Caliph al-Ma'mun founded the Bait-ul-Hikmat, or the "House of Wisdom," a center dedicated to study and the translation of books. Scholars at the House of Wisdom translated the works of the ancient Greeks and other non-Muslims, including Persians, Jews, Christians, and Indians. Caliph al-Ma'mun located the House of Wisdom in Madinat al-Salam, or "City of Peace,"

"Seeking knowledge is a duty upon every Muslim."
Prophet Muhammad

Archimedes

The School of Athens. This fresco by Italian artist Raphael was painted between 1509 and 1511 in the Apostolic Palace in the Vatican. Representing the spirit of Renaissance, this painting depicts philosophers and scientists of ancient Greece, like Plato and Aristotle (under the arch), Euclid (in the right bottom corner, drawing a geometric diagram), Ptolemy (next to Euclid, holding an earth sphere), Ibn Rushd (Averroes) wearing a turban and looking over the shoulder of Pythagorus (in the left bottom corner) etc.

Ptolemy

terpret the wisdom of the ancients. For example, Abd al-Masih-bin Abadalla Wa'ima al-Himsi, a scholar who translated several books by ancient Greek philosophers into Arabic, was a Christian from the city of Emessa, located in what is now Syria. Sahl ibn Bishr al-Israili, the scholar who translated Ptolemy's astronomical manual, *Mathematike Syntaxis*, or *The Mathematical Arrangement*, into Arabic was a Jew from Tabaristan, located in what is now Iran, and was known as al-Tabari.

Al-Tabari called Ptolemy's *Mathematike Syntaxis* "al-Majisti," meaning "The Great Book." Scholars who later translated *al-Majisti* into Latin transliterated al-Tabari's title as *Almagest*, giving it the name it is known by in the West. Years later, Ibn al-Haytham worked from al-Tabari's translation of *Mathematike Syntaxis* when he wrote commentaries on Ptolemy's book.

The most famous book to emerge from the golden age of Islamic translation is *Kitāb Alf Laylah Wa Laylah*, known in the West as *One Thousand and One Nights*. Early in the tenth century, a scholar named Abu 'Abd Allah ibn 'Abdus al-Jashyari began to translate stories from as far away as Persia, India, and China into Arabic. He gave the heroes of the exotic tales the Arabic names they are known by today, including Aladdin, Ali Baba, Scheherazade, and Sinbad. In some cases, al-Jash-

the new capital of the Abbasid Caliphate, which the Muslims had founded in 762 on the site of the village of Baghdad.

Drawn by Caliph al-Ma'mun's generous pay, scholars from throughout the Middle East, North Africa, India, and even parts of Europe traveled to Madinat al-Salam to work at the House of Wisdom. Scholars did not have to be Muslims in order to translate for Caliph al-Ma'mun. Christians, Jews, Persians, and Indians worked side by side with Muslims to in-

yari changed not only the names of the characters, but also the locations of their adventures.

After al-Jashyari's death, other Islamic scholars and storytellers continued to add to his collection until it contained the full 1,001 stories suggested by the title. According to a historian named Abu Al-husayn 'ali Ibn Al-husayn Al-mas'udi, by 947 al-Jashyari's collection of stories was "called by the people 'A Thousand

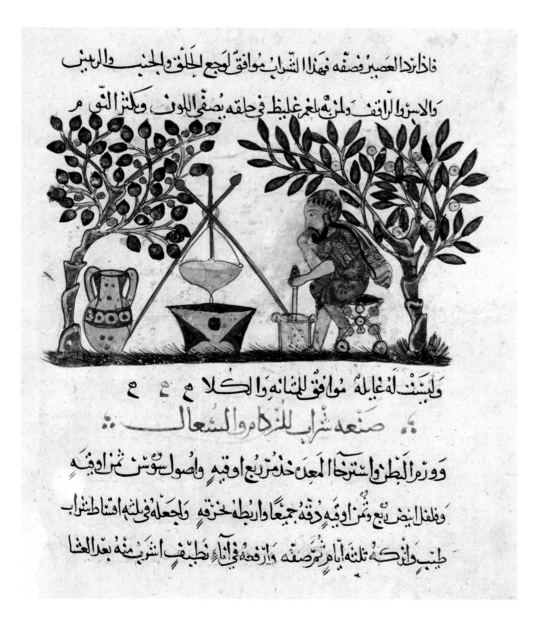

Physician preparing an elixir: folio from an Arabic manuscript of the *De Materia Medica* by Dioscorides (ca. 40–90 AD) .

A theatrical poster of Arabian nights by Buffalo, N.Y. : Courier Lith. Co., 1888].
Library of Congress.

One Thousand and One Nights as a young man or heard storytellers recite its tales of flying carpets, powerful genies, and magic caves.

As *One Thousand and One Nights* suggests, Islamic scholars did not merely collect and translate the works of other cultures. They absorbed the material and added to it, making it their own. This was true not only in literature, but also science and mathematics. Islamic advances in these areas changed the course of human history.

The most important breakthrough to come out of the House of Wisdom occurred around 825 when Muhammad ibn Musa al-Khwarizmi, a mathematician and astronomer, came across works by Hindu mathematicians that had been translated into Arabic. The Hindu mathematicians used a numbering system that included ten numerals: 1 through 9, and 0. At the time, much of the world used numbering systems, such as the one developed by the Romans, that did not include a zero as a placeholder. Impressed with the power and economy of the ten-digit, or decimal, numbering system, al-Khwarizmi began to use it in his astronomical calculations. He decided to explain the advantages of the Hindu system in a work he called *The Book of Addition and Subtraction According to the Hindu Calculation*. Adopted by everyone from scholars to merchants, al-Khwarizmi's numbering system swept through the Islamic world, eventually spreading to Europe and beond. Today the Hindu-Arabic numbering system is used worldwide.

Al-Khwarizmi was also responsible for the widespread acceptance of another important concept that changed the course of mathematics: algebra. This term came from the Latin translation of the Arabic words *al-jabr*, which appear in the title of al-Khwarizmi's book, *Al-Kitab al-mukhtasar fi hisab al-jabr wa'l-muqabala*, or *The Compendious Book on Calculation by Completion and Balancing*. In this book, al-Khwarizmi described a system of rules that could be used to solve certain mathematical problems. This book inspired another Muslim mathematician, Abu Kamil, who lived from 850 to 930, to create an even more advanced form of algebra. Eventually Abu Kamil's book made its way to Europe, where it inspired new generations of mathematicians to expand on Abu Kamil's concepts, advancing algebra even further.

As *One Thousand and One Nights* suggests, Islamic scholars did not merely collect and translate the works of other cultures. They absorbed the material and added to it, making it their own.

A page from Khwarizmi's *Algebra* (*Al-Kitab al-mukhtasar fi hisab al-jabr wa'l-muqabala,* or *The Compendious Book on Calculation by Completion and Balancing.*)

Algebra proved to have many practical uses. It helped Muslim leaders to divide up parcels of land, assess taxes, and distribute inheritances according to Islamic law. It also helped astronomers calculate the exact time to look for the new moon, marking the beginning of each month on the Islamic calendar. Since Muslims face the Kaaba—a building at the center of Islam's most sacred mosque in the city of Mecca, located in what is now Saudi Arabia—when they pray, they need to know the precise direction of the holy site. Islamic astronomers used algebra to calculate the precise direction for prayer, known as the *qibla,* for the faithful.

For these practical reasons, as well as out of a general love of knowledge, scholars working at the House of Wisdom were eager to share their findings with the rest of the world. In the age before the printing press, scribes had to copy the works of scholars by hand. Page by elegantly lettered page, the works of al-Khwarizmi, Abu Kamil, and other scholars spread throughout the Islamic world.

Some of these books found their way to libraries attached to mosques, the Islamic places of prayer and worship. Others were sold to wealthy individuals who maintained private libraries in their homes. It is likely that Ibn al-Haytham's father was one such person. That Ibn al-Haytham received an appointment to a government office as a young man suggests that his father held a senior post in the Abbasid Caliphate. The young Ibn al-Haytham may have encountered books by Islamic scholars and translations of the works of the ancient Greeks in his father's library.

Musa al-Khwarizmi

THE ISLAMIC CALENDAR

The Islamic calendar is used by Muslims to date historical events and determine the dates of Muslim holy days. The calendar is based on lunar cycles, with twelve lunar months and about 354 days in a year. Each month begins with the first sighting of the *hilal*, or lunar crescent, after sunset. The holiest month in the Islamic year is Ramadan, the ninth month, during which many Muslims fast during the day. Because weather conditions often do not allow for *hilal* sightings, some Muslims today use calendars worked out in advance, but traditionally the month does not officially begin until someone has physically seen the *hilal*. The importance of moon sightings in Islamic culture fueled interest in astronomy.

Pre-Islamic calendars had also used lunar months, but also added an extra month, called an intercalary month, so that one year would coincide with a solar year and the seasons would remain constant. Muhammad, however, expressly forbid the use of an intercalary month. Because an Islamic year is about eleven days shorter than a solar year, the dates of Islamic holy days shift accordingly each year. In 638 A.D., the second caliph, Umar ibn al-Khattab, dated the first year of the Islamic calendar to the year of the Hijra (corresponding to the Gregorian year 622 A.D.), when the Prophet Muhammad and his followers migrated from Mecca to Medina. Each Islamic year is designated as A.H., the initials for the Latin phrase *anno Hegirae* (in the year of the Hijra.) To roughly convert between Islamic years and Gregorian years, multiply the Islamic year by 0.97 and add 622. To convert between Gregorian years and Islamic years, subtract 622 and divide by 0.97.

Most of Ibn al-Haytham's early education likely took place at the mosque of Basra. Like other mosques throughout the Islamic world, the Basran mosque served not only as a place of worship, but also as a center for education. Modeled after Prophet Muhammad's original place of worship—the courtyard of his home in Medina—early mosques consisted of a large open area surrounded by columns that supported the roof. According to Muslim tradition, each teacher would take up a position by a pillar while his students sat on the floor in a semicircle around him. Dressed in flowing robes and leaning against the pillar, the teacher would read from a book, deliver a lecture, or challenge the students with questions. Teachers often held their classes by the same pillar year after year. In some mosques, the names of teachers were inscribed on the pillars where they taught. Many of those names still can be seen in mosques today.

Muslim students also would be required to participate in *munazarah*, or debates. As in modern debates, the participants in *munazarah* would pose difficult and controversial questions to each other. Answers were judged on their thoroughness and the soundness of their logic. We know from a title of one his books, *Replies to Seven Mathematical Questions Addressed to Me in Baghdad*, that Ibn al-Haytham participated in *munazarah* as an adult. His careful, precise writing style in this and other books reveals a nimble mind trained by the give-and-take of the *munazarah*.

Because books were difficult to produce in the tenth century, some teachers would have their students transcribe what they said during the lectures. After several weeks or months, the students would have produced several copies of the scholar's views. The teacher would then sign each book to mark the proficiency of the student, like a modern-day diploma. Using this method of dictation, known as *tariq-i-imla*, scholars increased the chances that copies of their lectures would circulate among scholars and their ideas would spread more quickly.

"The Lesson." Rudolphe
Ernst, an Austrian, portrays
a teacher of the Qur'an by
his post. Oil on canvas.
Early 1900s. Bridgeman
Art Library.

The teachers in the mosques concentrated on subjects such as religion, literature, grammar, and rhetoric that today would be grouped under the heading of the humanities. The subjects known as the ulum-al-taalim, or the sciences—including astronomy, mathematics, medicine, and physics—were not usually taught in the mosques. More often those subjects were discussed in the private homes of amateur scholars and other patrons of education.

According to an autobiographical sketch that Ibn al-Haytham wrote when he was sixty-three years old, he devoted much of his early education to theology, the study of the nature of God and religious truth. His theology teachers would have spent a great deal of time reading and explaining the Qur'an and the Hadith, a collection of the sayings of Prophet Muhammad. They also would have discussed how the Islamic scriptures applied to everyday practices, such as commerce, government, and law.

Although bound by tradition and the personal relationships that grew between teachers and pupils, education in Ibn al-Haytham's day was not as systematic as it is now. Students were not required to take specific courses or attend school at all. Those who wanted to study would choose a teacher and pay him a certain amount of money. Students were free to move from one teacher to another and change their course of study at any time. After years of studying theology, this is exactly what Ibn al-Haytham did. It was a decision that would change both the direction of his life and the course of science.

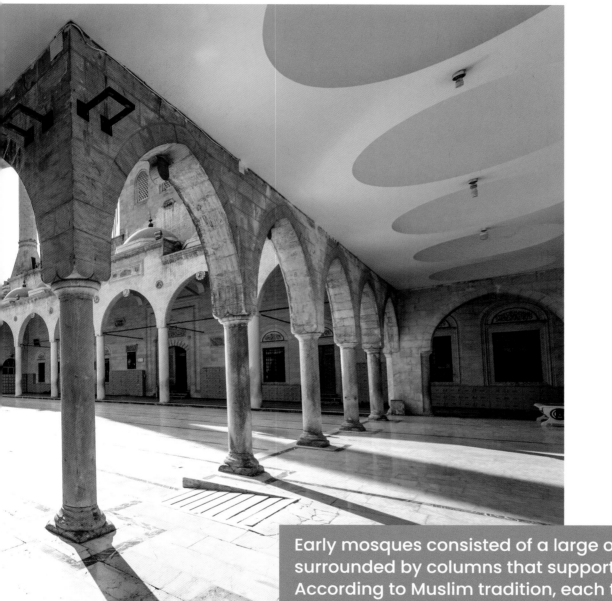

Early mosques consisted of a large open area surrounded by columns that supported the roof. According to Muslim tradition, each teacher would take up a position by a pillar while his students sat on the floor in a semicircle around him.

Mosque courtyard and silence; interior photo- Halil-ur-Rahman Mosque (Mosque Floor)

II

THE QUEST FOR KNOWLEDGE

A devout Muslim, Ibn al-Haytham spent most of his life trying to know and serve his God. "I decided to discover what it is that brings us closer to God, what pleases Him most, and what makes us submissive to His ineluctable Will,"[6] Ibn al-Haytham wrote in his autobiography. His restless and probing mind drove him to closely examine the doctrines of Islam. Convinced that "Truth is a unitary entity"[7] for all people, in all places, at all times, he also studied the theology of the ancient Greeks, especially Aristotle. While still a student, Ibn al-Haytham began to examine the views held by the members of different sects, or groups, within Islam. "From my very childhood I have been reflecting on various sects and their beliefs," he wrote in his autobiography. "Each sect," he noted, "has framed its opinions and beliefs according to the principles of its faith."[8]

The sects did not always agree about important issues. Two of the largest sects, the Shi'ah and the Sunni, disagreed about the rightful successor of Prophet Muhammad. The Shi'ah believed that Prophet Muhammad chose 'Ali ibn Abi Talib, his son-in-law and the father of his only surviving grandchildren, Hasan and Husayn, as his successor. The Sunni claimed, and still claim, that Prophet Muhammad designated no successor, but encouraged his followers to choose their leader by *shura*, or consultation.

The disagreements over Prophet Muhammad's successor led to other theological differences. Most Shi'ah believe that the twelve descendants of Prophet Muhammad, beginning with 'Ali, were special leaders known as the imam. According to Shi'ah theology, the imam were infallible, and they alone understood the true meaning of the Qur'an. After the death of the twelfth imam, most Shi'ah believe, other holy men, known as mujtahids, were given the responsibility of interpreting Islamic doctrine and law. The Sunni, by contrast, believe that matters of doctrine can be settled by *al-jama'ah*, or "the consolidated majority."[9] To this day, the Sunni and Shi'ah remain divided on these and other issues.

Tomb of Imam Ali, Najaf, Iraq.

The disagreements between the Sunni, the Shi'ah, and other Islamic sects, such as the Sufi and Mu'tazilah, troubled the young Ibn al-Haytham. He realized that if one belief was true, then a conflicting belief could not also be true; one of the beliefs must be false. False beliefs were dangerous, he reasoned, because they obscured the truth and led believers away from God. It was in the best interest of all believers, Ibn al-Haytham concluded, to identify which beliefs were true and which were false.

> **"I decided to discover what it is that brings us closer to God, what pleases Him most, and what makes us submissive to His ineluctable Will."**

Although still a young man, Ibn al-Haytham took it upon himself to identify and expose false beliefs, which he likened to evil enchantments. "Having gained an insight into the intellectual bases of the sects," he wrote, "I decided to dedicate myself to the search for truth so as to tear away the veil of superstitions and doubts, which an illusive vision has cast on people, and so that the doubting and the skeptical people may lift their gaze freed from the membrane of spell and skepticism."[10] The young theologian hoped that by revealing the truths behind the doctrines, he would be able to close the rifts that had opened between the sects.

After studying the various belief systems in depth, Ibn al-Haytham came to a startling conclusion. He decided that the differences between the sects were rooted not in doctrine, but in the backgrounds of the various believers. "I have ... begun to doubt the views of various sects," he wrote, "and I am now convinced that ... whatever differences exist between various sects are based not on the basic tenets of faith or the Ultimate Reality but on sociological content."[11] This revelation brought with it a sobering realization: His study of theology had not brought him any closer to understanding the true nature of God. His disappointment was still apparent forty-five years later. "I studied in considerable detail the beliefs of various sects, thoughts, and theological systems," he wrote in his autobiographical sketch, "but I failed to gain anything which could point the way to Reality."[12] The young scholar was frustrated. He had spent years on research that had led him nowhere. Worse, he did not know what to do next.

In his autobiography Ibn al-Haytham does not say how long this period of disappointment lasted, but he does explain how it came to an end: He discovered the works of the philosopher Aristotle. The words of the ancient Greek philosopher were a revelation to the young Islamic scholar. He found in Aristotle a kindred spirit and

> "I am now convinced that ... whatever differences exist between various sects are based not on the basic tenets of faith or the Ultimate Reality, but on sociological content."

an intellectual equal, a man whose methods and insights gave him a new purpose in life. "When I discovered what Aristotle had done," he later recalled, "I became engrossed in my desire to understand philosophy wholeheartedly."[13]

Aristotle's approach to understanding the world was broader than anything Ibn al-Haytham had encountered before. "Aristotle has discussed the nature of the physical world," he wrote. "He has analyzed causality and teleology, the celestial beings, plants and animals, Universe and Soul." What impressed Ibn al-Haytham most, however, was Aristotle's commitment to logic and reason. "He has analyzed the terminology of logic and has divided it into primary kinds," Ibn al-Haytham observed. "Furthermore, he has analyzed those aspects which are the material and elemental bases of reasoning, and he has described their classes.... This analysis is essential for his discussion of truth and falsehood."[14]

Never again would Ibn al-Haytham spend his time studying matters that were unknowable and unprovable. "I saw that I can reach the truth only through concepts whose matter are sensible things, and whose form is rational,"[15] he wrote. "I found such theories present in the logic, physics, and theology of Aristotle."[16]

ARISTOTLE

Aristotle was born in 384 B.C. in the ancient Macedonian city of Stageira. The son of a prominent doctor, Aristotle traveled to Athens at the age of eighteen to study under the great philosopher Plato at the Greek Academy. When Plato died in 344 B.C., Aristotle served for eight years as tutor to King Philip of Macedon's son, Alexander, who later conquered most of the Middle East and Southwest Asia. After Alexander had completed his studies, Aristotle returned to Athens to begin his own school of philosophy, known as the Lyceum, where he wrote most of his important treatises. Because Aristotle liked to give his philosophical lectures while walking about, his followers were known as Peripatetics, which means "walking."

Aristotle is one of the most important figures in Western thought. He wrote on poetry, rhetoric, politics, biology, physics, astronomy, logic, and a number of other subjects. Although his conclusions on physics fell into disrepute in the sixteenth and seventeenth centuries, Aristotle laid the foundation for scientific reasoning. He believed in the value of both empirical knowledge (knowledge gleaned from the senses) and logical knowledge (knowledge deduced by the mind).

Aristotle's teacher Plato had argued that the material world is but a series of imitations of ideal forms. Inquiry, therefore, should be a top-down, strictly deductive process. Aristotle also believed in logic, and wrote even more extensively on the subject than Plato had, but thought that inquiry should begin with study of the material world, and then proceed to deduction. This was a methodology that would be employed and refined by Ibn al-Haytham. Unlike Ibn al-Haytham, however, Aristotle did not believe in experimentation. He thought his observations alone would suffice.

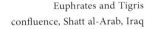

Euphrates and Tigris
confluence, Shatt al-Arab, Iraq

Islamic scholars sitting in a library discuss a book in this illustration from al-Hariri's *The Assemblies* written in the year 1237.

Equipped with Aristotle's outlook and techniques, Ibn al-Haytham renewed his commitment to better understanding the Creator and His universe. "It became my belief that for gaining access to the effulgence and closeness to God, there is no better way than that of searching for truth and knowledge,"[17] he wrote. Rather than studying the words of men, he would examine the works of God. "There are three disciplines which go to make philosophy: mathematics, physical sciences, and theology," Ibn al-Haytham declared. "As long as I live, I shall keep myself pressed into the service of these disciplines."[18]

Ibn al-Haytham could not have chosen a better place to embark on his journey of discovery than his own hometown of Basra. Located on the western bank of Shatt Al-Arab, the waterway that connects the Tigris and Euphrates rivers with the Persian Gulf, also known as the Arabian Gulf, Basra had grown from a small military outpost to a busy port city, teeming with a variety of cultures and beliefs. Merchants from Asia, Africa, and the islands of the Indian Ocean sailed to Basra to profit from its growing trade. A few of the foreign merchants decided to stay in Basra and make it their home. Small communities of Africans, Indians, Persians, and Malays flourished in the busy port city. These groups practiced their own religions and followed their own customs and traditions.

Not all of the visitors to Basra were merchants. Scholars on their way to the House of Wisdom in Baghdad often stayed as the guests of local patrons of learning. Sometimes the traveling scholars would be asked to lecture or to participate in a *munazarah*. Even if Ibn al-Haytham did not participate in such discussions himself, he heard about them from others and no doubt benefited from the vibrant intellectual atmosphere of his hometown.

Ibn al-Haytham began his pursuit of philosophy by reading as many of Aristotle's works as possible. When he finished reading one of Aristotle's books, he often would write a summary of it so students and other scholars could become familiar with the philosopher's views without having to read the entire work. According to a list Ibn al-Haytham compiled at age sixty-three, he had written at least thirteen abridgements, or summaries, of Aristotle's works. Even so, Ibn al-Haytham did not believe his work was done. "Should God out of his limitless bounty extend my life span and grant me time to pursue my studies," he wrote, "I shall condense two books by Aristotle, one on natural healing and the other on heaven and earth."[19]

As Ibn al-Haytham grew confident in his understanding of Aristotle's ideas, he began to not only summarize the works, but also to comment on them. In one treatise Ibn al-Haytham defended Aristotle's views on the nature of the cosmos from criticism raised by a philosopher named Yahya Nahhavi. Ibn al-Haytham followed this treatise with a second, more thorough defense of Aristotle's work. He also de-

Ibn al-Haytham studied the work of Ptolemy of Alexandria, who used trigonometry to predict the motions of the sun, moon, planets, and stars.

fended one of Aristotle's books from criticism by Abu Hashim, a leader of the Mu'tazilah sect.

Ibn al-Haytham did not confine himself to the study of philosophy. He began to investigate the physical sciences and higher mathematics as well. He soon discovered that he had a gift for mathematics.

Ibn al-Haytham began his mathematical studies by reading the works of Euclid, a Greek mathematician born around 300 bce. Euclid lived and worked in Alexandria, the ancient capital of Egypt founded by the Greek conqueror Alexander the Great in 332 bce. Euclid's most famous book, *Elements*, was the best introduction to geometry and number theory available in Ibn al-Haytham's day. As he did after reading Aristotle's works, Ibn al-Haytham summarized and condensed Euclid's writings. He also analyzed them. In one book, he categorized the theorems and problems discussed by Euclid. In another, which he called "a thesaurus of mathematics," Ibn al-Haytham made discoveries of his own. "I have taken Euclid as the guide with regard to geometrical and numerical laws," he wrote of his thesaurus. "I have solved various geometrical problems and have explained the numerical problems by means of equations. I have also deviated from the postures adopted by the previous exponents of algebra."[20]

The castle of
Qaitbay, the
Mamluk Sultan of
Egypt. 15th century.

Confident of his abilities, Ibn al-Haytham delved into the works of other ancient Greek mathematicians. He studied the works of Archimedes, the Greek mathematician and inventor who was born in 290 bce in Syracuse, on the island of Sicily, off the coast of Italy. In his exploration of geometry, Archimedes grouped angles into three basic kinds. Ibn al-Haytham reflected on this idea and wrote a commentary criticizing the logic Archimedes had used to come to his conclusions.

Ibn al-Haytham also studied the work of Claudius Ptolemy, an Egyptian of Greek descent who lived and worked in Alexandria around 150 ce. In his most famous work, an astronomical manual called *Almagest*, Ptolemy used trigonometry, a branch of mathematics devoted to the study of the functions of angles, to predict the motions of the sun, moon, planets, and stars. Ibn al-Haytham was fascinated by this work and produced summary of it, but he was not satisfied with his work. "I have not been able to derive any mathematical law of import from *Almagest*, which I have abridged and on which I have compiled a commentary," Ibn al-Haytham wrote. "If I am vouchsafed a longer life by the grace of God, I shall write another commentary which shall embody the algebraic and other mathematical disciplines thoroughly."[21]

Ibn al-Haytham would live many more years, but his life was about to take a surprising new direction—one that threatened to keep him from writing his commentary on the *Almagest*, his summaries of Aristotle's works, or any other new books.

As he did after reading Aristotle's works, Ibn al-Haytham summarized and condensed Euclid's writings.

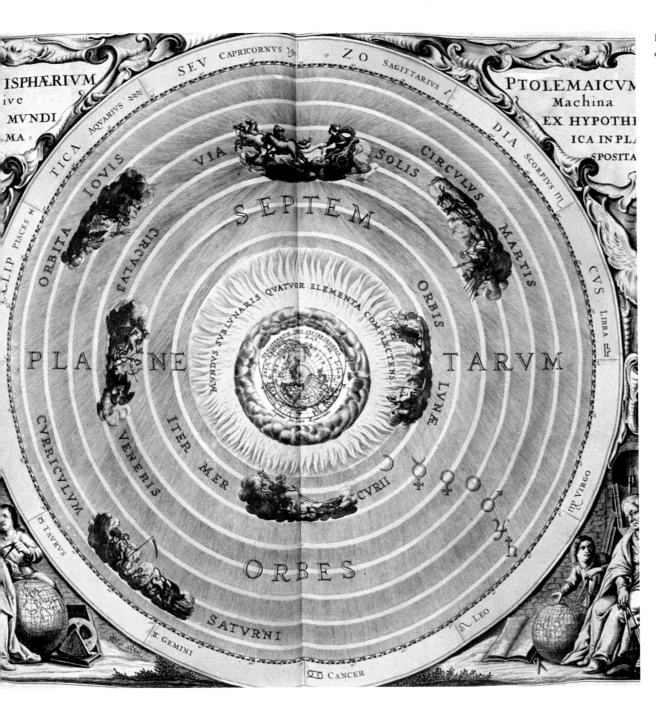

Ptolemy's diagram of the universe

III

"MADNESS"

Just as Ibn al-Haytham began using reason and mathematics to unlock the secrets of the universe, he was appointed to a position within the government of Basra that most young men in the Abbasid Caliphate would have been delighted to receive. A job in the government provided a good income, a certain amount of prestige, and a lifetime of security. Ibn al-Haytham, however, feared that his duties would leave little time to study mathematics and philosophy.

The main source of information about Ibn al-Haytham's appointment to a government office comes from *Tabaqāt al-aṭibbā*, a biographical dictionary compiled around 1250 by an Islamic historian named Ibn Abī Usaybi'ah. In addition to accounts of events in Ibn al-Haytham's life, Ibn Abī Usaybi'ah provides a copy of Ibn al-Haytham's autobiographical sketch. He also repeats a story he heard from a scholar named 'Alam al-Dīn Qaysar ibn Abi 'l-Qāsim ibn Musāfir, more commonly known as Qaysar, who was born in Upper Egypt in 1178 and died in Damascus, Syria, in 1251. According to Qaysar, Ibn al-Haytham was named a vizier, or high official, within the government.

Qaysar did not reveal why Ibn al-Haytham received this appointment. It is likely, however, that Ibn al-Haytham's family played a role in securing to post for him. Such appointments often were given to families that had proven themselves to high officials through years of loyal service. That Ibn al-Haytham received an excellent education in his youth suggests that his family was well off financially and

The Ziggurat of Ur. Basra, where Ibn al-Haytham was born and raised, is located in an area where some of the oldest examples of ancient civilizations still stand. Built during c. 2100 BCE (Early Bronze Age), this temple is only about two hours north of Basra. It was built as a step pyramid that reached a height of 30 m. in its original form.

possibly held positions in the government. Education was not free in the Abbasid Caliphate, and poor families could not afford to pay teachers. Ibn al-Haytham's family, by contrast, could afford for their son to study for many years. They may have supported his education because they knew that he was in line to receive a government post.

It is also possible that Ibn al-Haytham sought the appointment himself, perhaps because he had gotten married or was planning to get married and wanted to support his family. The evidence for Ibn al-Haytham's marriage comes from an inscription in the oldest surviving copy of his *Kitāb al-Manāzir*, or *Book of Optics*. The person who copied the manuscript gives his name as Ahmad ibn Muhammad ibn Ja'far al-'Askarī. He states that he is the son-in-law of the author of the book. If Ibn al-Haytham had a son-in-law, then he must have had a daughter. If he had a daughter, then he most likely was married, since few Muslim children were born outside of wedlock in the tenth century.

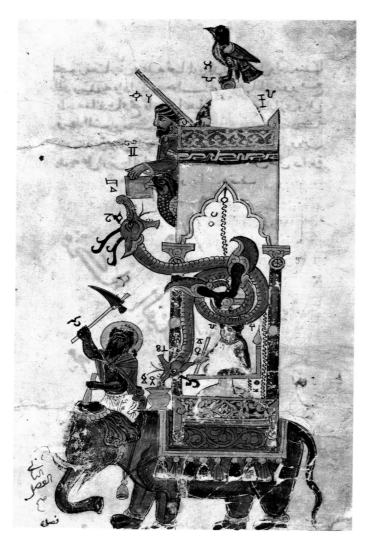

The elephant clock of Al-Jazari.
One of Ibn al-Haytham's books was *On the Construction of the Water Clock*, and the scale of the project in this book suggests that it arose from his duties as an officer of the government. To have an idea about his project, it may be helpful to study Al-Jazari's (d. 1206) manuscript *Kitab fi marifat al-hiyal al-handasiyya'* (The Book of Knowledge of Ingenious Mechanical Devices), which shows this elephant water clock that accurately recorded time with an automaton striking a cymbal and a robotic bird chirping.

Qaysar did not specify what kind of duties Ibn al-Haytham performed as vizier. Some historians believe he was a financial minister. Ibn al-Haytham later wrote a book entitled *On Business Arithmetic*, showing that he was familiar with financial issues. Other historians believe that Ibn al-Haytham was a civil engineer, in charge of public works projects such as the building of roads, bridges, and buildings. Ibn al-Haytham wrote several books that show a knowledge of civil engineering and surveying, including *Determination of the Altitudes of Mountains*, *Determination of the Height of the Pole with the Greatest Precision*, *On the Altitudes of Triangles*, and *On the Principles of Measurement*. Three hundred years after Ibn al-Haytham died, a Fatimid scholar still praised his *On the Principles of Measurement*. "This work is extremely useful for computing the revenue, the division of land, and the measurement of buildings,"[22] the scholar wrote.

Further evidence that Ibn al-Haytham may have been a civil engineer comes from another of his books, *On the Construction of the Water Clock*. This book was not about the kind of clock that would sit on a desk or table, but a large piece of machinery that would be placed in a public area, often near the gate of a mosque. Ibn al-Haytham probably would not have undertaken the task of building such a large and important timepiece on his own. The scale of the project suggests that it arose from his duties as an officer of the government.

As his book about the water clock suggests, Ibn al-Haytham was fascinated by hydrodynamics, the motion of fluids. He wrote at least two other books on the subject, including a work about canals and dams. He also spent some time studying the ebb and flow of the Nile River in Africa.

Ibn al-Haytham claimed that he could build a system of dams, levees, and canals that would prevent the Nile from overflowing in the fall and would preserve its waters for irrigation during the hot, dry summer.

Rising from the shores of Lake Victoria in Uganda and flowing northward 4,132 miles (6,650 km) to the Mediterranean Sea, the Nile is the longest river in the world. Swollen by heavy summer rains near the equator, the ancient Nile rose until it overflowed its banks in Egypt in October. The annual flooding of the Nile deposited rich, dark silt across the Egyptian floodplain, allowing farmers to cultivate the same land year after year without depleting the soil. The flood levels varied from year to year, however, causing serious problems for the Egyptians. Too little flooding resulted in crop failure and famine; too much killed livestock and spread disease. Once the Nile had crested, its water level dropped rapidly through the late fall and winter and continued to ebb through the spring, leaving less water for irrigation.

According to a twelfth-century historian named ʿAlī ibn Zayd al-Bayhaqī, Ibn al-Haytham wrote "a book on civil engineering in which he discussed the possibility of offsetting the shortage of water in the Nile."[23] Ibn Abī Usaybiʿah reported that Ibn al-Haytham claimed that he could build a system of dams, levees, and canals that would prevent the Nile from overflowing in the fall and would preserve its waters for irrigation during the hot, dry summer. "Had I been in Egypt," Ibn al-Haytham declared, "I could have done something to regulate the Nile so that the people could derive benefit (out of its water) at its ebb and flow."[24]

As much as these practical issues may have interested Ibn al-Haytham, they did not displace his love of pure learning. He longed to return to the study of philosophy and mathematics. His government position made this impossible, however. Qaysar reports that Ibn al-Haytham thought about resigning from his government post, but this was not realistic. He had been appointed by a high official of the government, probably the governor of Basra. Resigning from his post would have insulted the person who appointed him and reflected badly on his own family. He could have run away, but this also would have brought dishonor to his family.

The Nile rises from the shores of Lake Victoria in Uganda and flows northward 4,132 miles to the Mediterranean Sea. The city of Cairo stretches along this river, which has been serving as a source of life for nature and human beings. Ibn al-Haytham made plans to regulate the Nile for more benefit at its ebb and flow.

According to Qaysar, Ibn al-Haytham came up with an unusual plan to escape his duties: He pretended to be insane. At first Ibn al-Haytham's superiors were suspicious of this ruse. They relieved the young vizier of his duties, but they continued to observe him. Convinced the illness was real, they removed him from office.

It is possible that Ibn al-Haytham was not faking his illness. In his autobiography, Ibn al-Haytham makes an intriguing statement about the inner forces that shaped his life and career. "I am not aware of the feelings, thoughts, and sensations which have guided me since my childhood," he wrote. "Call it what you may—a matter of chance, or intuition vouchsafed by Almighty God, or madness. You may attribute the source of my inspiration to any of the three."[25]

It is possible that Ibn al-Haytham claimed to be insane to set himself apart from other scholars or to make himself seem especially inspired. In his writings, however, Ibn al-Haytham comes across as a humble person, giving credit to others and deflecting attention away from himself. It is hard to imagine that he would

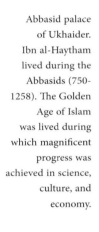

Abbasid palace of Ukhaider. Ibn al-Haytham lived during the Abbasids (750-1258). The Golden Age of Islam was lived during which magnificent progress was achieved in science, culture, and economy.

have tried to enhance his reputation with false claims. He took great care to avoid overstatement in his books; there is no reason to think he did otherwise in his autobiography.

From what is known about his personality and beliefs, it also would have been out of character for Ibn al-Haytham to mislead government officials about his mental state. He often said that pursing the truth was the most important thing in life. Deceiving the government about his mental fitness would not have been a small breach of the truth; it would have been an elaborate hoax that would have to have spanned months, if not years. It would have required not just one lie, but an endless stream of them. Such a deception would have affected not only Ibn al-Haytham, but also many people close to him, including his family, friends, and associates. He would have had to have fooled them all, or else let them in on his secret, making them accomplices in his scheme to defraud the government and putting them at risk of punishment. Nothing in Ibn al-Haytham's life suggests that he was capable of such selfishness or dishonesty.

Ibn al-Haytham often said that pursuing the truth was the most important thing in life.

A few years after being dismissed from his government appointment, Ibn al-Haytham again showed signs of mental instability. Mental illness is difficult if not impossible to cure, and recurrences are common. If Ibn al-Haytham had shown signs of mental illness only once, he might well have been faking his symptoms. However, the fact that he experienced a relapse suggests his problem was real. One possibility is that Ibn al-Haytham was autistic. Autism is a brain development disorder characterized by impairments in social interaction and communication. It often involves restricted and repetitive behavior. There are many degrees of autism, from mild to severe. As a result, mental health professionals refer to autism as a spectrum of disorders.

Caliph Al-Ma'mun (r. 813-833) is sending an envoy to Byzantine Emperor Theophilos. Al-Ma'mun established the Bayt al-Hikma (The House of Wisdom) where ancient texts were translated into Arabic. Al-Ma'mun loved learning, and it is told that after a battle he won, he asked the Byzantine Emperor a copy of Ptolemy's *Almagest* as a tribute.

One autism spectrum disorder that seems to fit Ibn al-Haytham's life story is known as Asperger's syndrome, named for the Austrian pediatrician Hans Asperger. In 1944, Asperger described children in his practice who appeared to have normal intelligence but lacked nonverbal communication skills and failed to demonstrate empathy with their peers. Asperger's syndrome is characterized by traits that could have been interpreted in the tenth and eleventh centuries as signs of madness. These traits include a limited but intense range of interests, especially specific intellectual areas; difficulty in social relationships, especially responding appropriately to others; problems communicating, such as difficulty making conversation or understanding other people.

According to his biographers, Ibn al-Haytham's mental problems surfaced when he was appointed to positions of responsibility. In his government posts, he would have had to interact with others and follow a routine. His inability to function in this environment is consistent with Asperger's syndrome. He seemed to function normally when he was on his own, giving rise to the idea that he faked his illness to pursue his studies. But the ability to function at a high level when alone is also consistent with Asperger's syndrome. It is worth noting that early in his career, Ibn al-Haytham became frustrated with theology, which involved people and opinions, and turned toward science and mathematics, which are more objective and provable. He wrote more than two hundred books and treatises, revealing the workaholism that is associated with Asperger's syndrome. He also was a voracious reader. It could even be said he had a mania for books, another trait shared by persons with Asperger's. In addition, Ibn al-Haytham's writings are not only careful and thorough, but also long and repetitive, almost to the point of obsessiveness—a possible sign of high functioning autism.

Perhaps most strikingly, one of the hallmarks of Asperger's syndrome is a rejection of established methods of learning and knowledge. Many persons with Asperger's syndrome are not good students. They tend to reject existing systems and replace them with their own. As a young man, Ibn al-Haytham did not simply accept Shi'ah or Sunni doctrine. He questioned them, believing he could discover "the ultimate Reality." Likewise, in science, he criticized existing theories and systems. This rejection of authorities would eventually lead Ibn al-Haytham to create his own method of knowing and judging the truth, one that involved experimentation, the hallmark of modern science.

Real or fake, Ibn al-Haytham's mental difficulties allowed him to escape the drudgery of his government job. His freedom restored, he returned to the pursuits he loved—mathematics, geometry, and philosophy. At last, it seemed, he would be able to write his commentary on the *Almagest*. Once again, however, Ibn al-Haytham's life took an unexpected turn. One day around 1010, a stranger showed up at Ibn al-Haytham's door. The visitor bore a message from Al-Hākim Bi-amr Allah, the sixth ruler of the Fatimid Caliphate of Egypt. Al-Hākim had learned of Ibn al-Haytham's statements about taming the Nile. The Fatimid leader wanted to discuss the Abbasid scholar's plan in person. Ibn al-Haytham was to come to Egypt immediately.

Ibn al-Haytham's writings are not only careful and thorough, but also long and repetitive, almost to the point of obsessiveness—a possible sign of high functioning autism.

Fountain of Ibn Tulun Mosque in Cairo

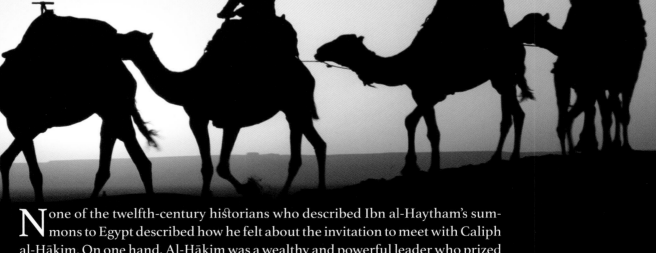

IV

TO EGYPT

None of the twelfth-century historians who described Ibn al-Haytham's summons to Egypt described how he felt about the invitation to meet with Caliph al-Hākim. On one hand, Al-Hākim was a wealthy and powerful leader who prized learning. He patronized scholars such as astronomer Ibn Yūnus and built the Dār al-'Ilm library in Cairo, which rivaled the House of Wisdom in Baghdad. He built several mosques and was considered a holy man. The Isma'ili sect of Shi'ah Muslims believed that Al-Hākim, whose full name, Al-Hākim Bi-amr Allah, means "Ruler by God's Command," was a descendant of Prophet Muhammad. Since Ibn al-Haytham had voiced his desire to control the flooding of the Nile, he no doubt felt honored to be asked for his help by such an important figure. If he succeeded in taming the Nile, Al-Hākim would reward him generously.

ORIGINS OF THE FATIMID DYNASTY

Al-Hakim Bi-amr Allah (The Mad Caliph) ruled over the Fatimid dynasty, which extended over most of North Africa from 910 to 1171. The word Fatimid is derived from "Fatima," who was the Prophet Muhammad's daughter and the husband of 'Ali ibn Abi Talib, the man Shi'ah Muslims consider to be the rightful successor to Muhammad. The Fatimids belonged to the Shi'ah sect named the Isma'ili.

All Shi'ah believe that the succession of the caliphate should pass through the descendants of Fatima and 'Ali, but an issue arose after the death of Ja'far al-Sadiq, the sixth Shi'ah Imam. Both of al-Sadiq's two sons, Musa al-Kazim and Isma'il bin Jafar, had claims to become the seventh Imam. Most Shi'ah supported Musa and his progeny, up through the twelfth Imam; they are thus known as Twelvers and today constitute about eighty percent of all Shi'ah. Isma'il's supporters are known as Isma'ilis, or Seveners, because they believe Isma'il was the last (and seventh) rightful Imam. The Isma'ili were a small but dedicated group that established power in Yemen and eventually sent emissaries to conquer North Africa.

The first Fatimid caliph, Ubayd Allah al-Mahdi Billah, assumed power in 909. He claimed to have descended from Fatima and 'Ali, through Isma'il, although many Muslim theologians, both then and now, disputed this claim. The Fatimids were the first power in the Middle East to seriously challenge the power of the Sunni Abbasid Caliphate in two hundred years. They built up a flourishing trade empire that included ports on both the Mediterranean and Red Seas. In 970, when Ibn al-Haytham was just five years old, they conquered Egypt and relocated the capital to Cairo. Caliph al-Hakim was Ubayd's great-great-great grandson.

Al-Hakim Mosque, Cairo. Al-Hakim completed the mosque and opened it for full service in 1013. The construction was started in 990 by Al-Muiz, the father of Al-Hakim.

Fresco of the Fatimid caliph Al-Hakim, dating to the 11th century AD.
(By Loaka 1. Wikimedia Commons)

On the other hand, Al-Hākim was known as a strange and capricious leader. For example, he once ordered the slaughter of all the dogs in Cairo because their barking annoyed him. He could be cruel to human beings as well. Shortly after coming to power, he ordered the destruction of the city of al-Fustat, near Cairo, the capital of the Fatimid dynasty. Throughout his reign, he persecuted Sunni Muslims, Jews, and Christians. For these and other reasons, Al-Hākim was called "The Mad Caliph." Even if Ibn al-Haytham was pleased with the prospect of putting his ideas into action, he probably had misgivings about serving such a violent and unpredictable leader.

Ibn al-Haytham must have had concerns about giving up the study of philosophy and mathematics once again. He knew that building a dam on the Nile would take years, if not an entire lifetime. If he accepted this monumental task, he might have to put off his studies indefinitely. Ibn al-Haytham had resented his duties in the government of Basra. His duties in Egypt would be even more demanding.

Even if Ibn al-Haytham had second thoughts about going to Egypt, there was not much he could do about it. Declining such an offer would have insulted one of the most powerful men in the Islamic world. Al-Hākim easily could have responded to such a refusal with violence or other punishment. The Fatimid ruler certainly had the means to enforce his wishes, even in the faraway Abbasid Caliphate.

Pleased with the invitation or not, Ibn al-Haytham left for Egypt late in 1010 or early in 1011. He probably traveled north along the Tigris River to Baghdad; west toward

Damascus, entering the Fatimid Caliphate; south through Jerusalem; west across the Sinai Peninsula; and finally into Egypt—a total distance of 1,400 miles (2,253 km). His journey would have taken between two and four months, depending on whether he traveled by foot, donkey, horse, or camel. If he stopped in various cities along the way—to visit the House of Wisdom in Baghdad, for example—the journey would have taken even longer. Two medieval historians, 'Ali ibn Zayd al-Bayhaqī and Jamāl al-Dīn ibn al-Qiftī, described what happened when Ibn al-Haytham arrived in Egypt. The two accounts differ, but both agree that Ibn al-Haytham met Al-Hākim face to face.

The earliest account comes from 'Ali ibn Zayd al-Bayhaqī, a historian who died about thirty years after Ibn al-Haytham did. According to Al-Bayhaqī, when Ibn al-Haytham arrived in Cairo he made his way to an inn. After resting for a few days, he received word that Al-Hākim was outside the gate of the inn, asking for him. When Ibn al-Haytham reached the street, he found the caliph seated on a donkey that wore a silver-plated harness. A short man, Ibn al-Haytham climbed up on a bench to speak with the caliph eye-to-eye. He presented the Fatimid leader with his treatise about building a dam on the Nile and began to explain his plan. Al-Hākim listened as he looked through the Abbasid scholar's book.

A satellite view of the Nile, visible as the green line in Egypt and forming a delta on the shores of the Mediterranean in the north.

When Ibn al-Haytham had finished speaking, the caliph glanced up. "You are wrong," said Al-Hākim, "because the expenses likely to be incurred on the project are in excess of the gains."[26] To emphasize his disappointment with the plan, Al-Hākim ordered his guards to destroy the bench on which Ibn al-Haytham had stood. "At this, Abu Ali [Ibn al-Haytham] was overcome by dire fear for his own life and fled the same night from Cairo," Al-Bayhaqī wrote. "At long last he reached Syria and sought refuge with one of the Syrian nobles."[27]

Jamāl al-Dīn ibn al-Qiftī's account differs from Al-Bayhaqī's in many ways. According to Al-Qiftī, Al-Hākim was so eager to meet Ibn al-Haytham that he rode out to the village of al-Khandaq to greet him. It was there that Ibn al-Haytham described his ideas for controlling the Nile. In Al-Qiftī's account, Al-Hākim did not ridicule the plan. On the contrary, the Fatimid leader was so impressed by Ibn al-Haytham and his ideas that he pledged to give the Abbasid scholar all of the workers and money he would need to complete the project.

With Al-Hākim's backing, Ibn al-Haytham traveled six hundred miles (966 km) south along the Nile to the village of Al-Janādil, near present-day Aswān, where he proposed to build his dam. Along the way, Ibn al-Haytham's party crossed the Nile and visited the pyramids of the ancient Egyptian pharaohs. Ibn al-Haytham was impressed by the precision and scale of these huge monuments. He had never seen anything like them, and he began to wonder about the engineers who built them. If they were capable of creating these massive works, he reasoned, then they must have been capable of building a dam on the Nile. That they did not do so concerned him.

Once Ibn al-Haytham reached Al-Janādil, he saw that he was right in thinking it was an ideal place to build a dam. Granite banks rise from each side of the river, forming a natural channel. Ibn al-Haytham realized that if workers could block the north end of the channel with a stone dam, the water would not be able to flow around it. Held in by the granite banks, the water would rise behind the dam, forming a lake.

The problems arose when Ibn al-Haytham measured the opening between the banks. The river itself is 1,800 feet (549 m) wide, but the opening in the granite is more than 3,200 wide feet (975 m) at ground level—four times wider than the base of the Great Pyramid of Khufu. The banks do not rise straight up from ground level, but instead slope away from the river. At a point 360 feet (110 m) above the river, the banks stand more than 12,000 feet (3,658 m) apart—sixteen times the width of the Great Pyramid. Ibn al-Haytham realized that the scope of the project exceeded the resources at his command. Nine hundred years after Ibn al-Haytham surveyed the site, the Egyptian government built a dam across the Nile on the very spot that Ibn al-Haytham had proposed. The twentieth-century builders used nearly 58 million cubic yards (44.3 million cubic m) of material to construct the Aswan High Dam, roughly seventeen times the amount of material ancient builders used to build the Great Pyramid.

Ibn al-Haytham traveled six hundred miles south along the Nile to the village of Al-Janadil where he proposed to build his dam.

Aswan High Dam, Egypt. Opened in 1970, nine centuries after Ibn al-Haytham surveyed the site, the Egyptian government built a dam across the Nile on the very spot that Ibn al-Haytham had proposed.

61

Considering Al-Hākim's reputation as a violent and unstable man, Ibn al-Haytham probably had doubts about telling him the bad news. Under the circumstances, it would not have been surprising if Ibn al-Haytham had fled from Egypt, fearing for his life, as Al-Bayhaqī suggested he did. According to Al-Qiftī, however, Ibn al-Haytham traveled to Cairo, met with Al-Hākim, and admitted that his plan would not work.

Al-Hākim did not react to Ibn al-Haytham's report as a Mad Caliph might have been expected to. On the contrary, Al-Hākim took the news calmly. Rather than punishing Ibn al-Haytham for his failure, Al-Hākim offered him a position in his government. According to Al-Qiftī, Ibn al-Haytham accepted the post "out of fear, not desire."[28]

Al-Qiftī states that not long after accepting the appointment, Ibn al-Haytham began to have second thoughts about serving Al-Hākim. The Abbasid scholar feared that the caliph would have a change of heart and order his punishment, perhaps even his execution. Ibn al-Haytham also may have viewed this government job the same way he viewed his job in Basra—as an impediment to his own research. Whatever the reason, Al-Qiftī states that Ibn al-Haytham sought a way out of his new post. According to the biographer, Ibn al-Haytham employed the same ruse he had used in Basra: He once again pretended to be mad.

> Al-Hakim placed Ibn al-Haytham under house arrest, confining him to a single house or room within Cairo.

It is worth noting that while Al-Qiftī and Al-Bayhaqī both report that Ibn al-Haytham escaped a government post by pretending to be insane, they did not agree on where this happened. Al-Bayhaqī says it occurred in Basra; Al-Qiftī says it occurred in Egypt. Neither historian says it happened twice. Since Al-Bayhaqī died one hundred years before Al-Qiftī did, it is possible that Al-Qiftī borrowed the insanity story from him and transferred it to Egypt. It is also possible that both accounts are true; Ibn al-Haytham may have pretended to be insane in Egypt precisely because the ruse had worked so well in Basra. However, it would have been more difficult to pull off such a hoax in Cairo than it was in Basra. Caliph al-Hākim was a brilliant man, and he surrounded himself with intelligent advisors. Fooling everyone in Al-Hākim's court would have been extremely difficult. It also would have been much more dangerous to attempt the hoax in Egypt than it would have been in Basra. Al-Hākim's violent history suggests he would not have hesitated to severely punish or even execute anyone who tried to fool him.

It is also possible that neither episode was staged. If Ibn al-Haytham had an autism spectrum disorder, the symptoms would have surfaced again when Al-Hākim placed him in a position of responsibility. Whatever the cause of Ibn al-Haytham's mental problems, Caliph al-Hakim handled the situation differently than the officials in Basra did. Instead of giving Ibn al-Haytham a leave of absence, Al-Hākim placed him under house arrest, confining him to a single house or room within Cairo. The caliph also took away Ibn al-Haytham's possessions. Al-

Qiftī's account does not specify how Al-Hākim enforced Ibn al-Haytham's confinement. Presumably he stationed guards outside the residence and had servants take food to the prisoner.

Days faded into weeks, weeks in months, and months into years as Ibn al-Haytham remained confined to a dwelling in Cairo. Stripped of his possessions, he could neither read nor write. Yet his mind was not necessarily dormant. Prisoners have been known to do amazing things to keep their minds occupied. Some have composed poems and even entire books and committed them to memory. Others have scratched writings and drawings into the walls of their cells. Given how active Ibn al-Haytham's mind was, it seems unlikely that he did nothing during the years that he held under house arrest. In fact, his confinement may have led to the greatest breakthrough of his career.

V

THE SCHOLAR OF CAIRO

The first device used for projecting an image onto a flat surface was known in Europe as the camera obscura. This term was derived from two Latin words: *camera*, meaning room or chamber, and *obscura*, meaning darkened. The original camera obscura was just that: a darkened room with a small opening, or aperture, that allowed light to shine onto a wall or screen. The light on the surface formed a color image—upside down and backwards—of whatever was outside the room, across from the aperture. Although the term camera obscura is Latin, the invention is not. It was described in *Kitāb al-Manāzir*, or *Book of Optics*, by Ibn al-Haytham.

The first device used for projecting an image onto a flat surface was known in Europe as the camera obscura. Although the term camera obscura is Latin, the invention is not. It was described in *Kitāb al-Manāzir*, or *Book of Optics*, by Ibn al-Haytham.

important work. In this book the Abbasid scholar corrected misconceptions about vision and light that scholars had believed for centuries. For example, the ancient Greeks believed that human beings were able to see because the eyes sent out rays that sensed objects. Ibn al-Haytham showed that the opposite was true: Vision occurs when rays of light enter the eye and stimulate the optic nerve. It was the first time in history that a person had accurately described the mechanics of vision. Ibn al-Haytham did not stop there, however. Building on the work of earlier scholars such as Aristotle, Euclid, Ptolemy, Theon of Alexandria, and Ya'qub ibn Ishaq as-Sabah al-Kindi, Ibn al-Haytham introduced a unified theory of light, correctly

describing its propagation, reflection, and refraction. *Book of Optics* remained the leading source of knowledge about optics for the next five hundred years.

> Ibn al-Haytham introduced a unified theory of light, correctly describing its propagation, reflection, and refraction.

The most important thing about *Book of Optics* is not the discoveries it contains but the way in which Ibn al-Haytham arrived at and supported those discoveries. He was the first person to systematically construct devices—such as the camera obscura—to test hypotheses and verify the accuracy of his findings. By using concrete, physical experiments to test hypotheses, Ibn al-Haytham helped establish the modern scientific method.

Book of Optics was not Ibn al-Haytham's first book about vision. In the introduction to *Book of Optics*, Ibn al-Haytham states that he wrote a treatise on optics earlier in his career. This work probably was a commentary on another book, such as Ptolemy's *Optics*. Ibn al-Haytham states that he "followed persuasive methods of reasoning" in his earlier work, but he did not test his hypotheses with what he called "true demonstrations." Ibn al-Haytham wrote that the lack of experimental proof was such an enormous flaw that anyone who came across the earlier work should disregard it.

At some point, Ibn al-Haytham came up with a new way to test and prove the facts about optics. How did this breakthrough occur? One clue emerges from the text of *Book of Optics*: It is a very solitary book. In it Ibn al-Haytham describes dozens of experiments, but only one—an experiment using a wooden block drilled with two holes to let light into a room—calls for the use of an assistant. The rest of the experiments are designed to be carried out by one person. The objects used in the experiments are few and simple: bare walls, stopped-up windows, screens, lamps, and tubes. The entire work has a feeling of having been composed in an empty room. Perhaps it was. It is possible that the world's first camera obscura was a prison cell in Cairo.

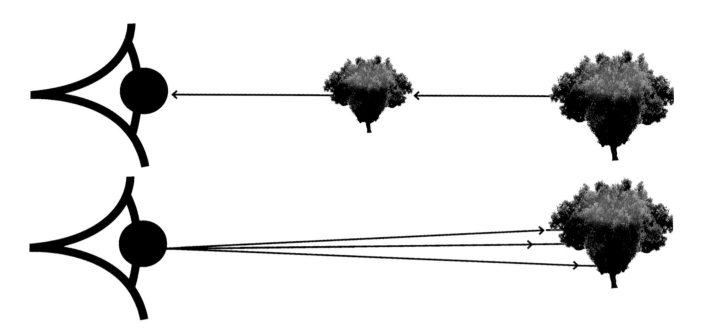

This diagram illustrates two ancient theories of vision that al-Haytham disagreed with in his *Book of Optics*. The first theory by Aristotle and his followers states that "vision is effected by a form which comes from the visible object to the eye" (top). The second theory, primarily advanced by Ptolemy and Euclid, states that "vision is effected by a ray which issues from the eye to the visible object" (bottom).

Ibn al-Haytham left no record of what he did for the years that Al-Qiftī says he was under house arrest. If, as Al-Qiftī says, Al-Hākim took away Ibn al-Haytham's possessions, the Abbasid scholar would not have had any of the books he brought to Egypt. As a result, he would not have been able to write his long-deferred commentary on the *Almagest* or commentaries on any other books. If he was not allowed to go outside, he would not have been able to observe enough of the night sky to write about astronomy. He would, however, have been able to watch the sky lighten at dawn, observe shafts of sunlight cut through his room in the afternoon, and ponder the light given off by an oil lamp in the evening. It is possible that Ibn al-Haytham realized how to conduct "true demonstrations relating to all objects of vision,"[29] as he describes his task in *Book of Optics*, during his long imprisonment. If his guards allowed him to have writing materials, he may have written some or all of *Book of Optics* during his confinement in Cairo.

Ibn al-Haytham begins *Book of Optics* by discussing the two theories of vision that had been circulating since the time of the ancient Greeks. The first theory, advanced by Aristotle and his followers, whom Ibn al-Haytham calls "the physicists"—states that "vision is effected by a form which comes from the visible object to the eye." The second theory, primarily advanced by Ptolemy and Euclid, whom Ibn al-Haytham calls "the mathematicians," states that "vision is effected by a ray which issues from the eye to the visible object." "These two notions," Ibn al-Haytham wrote, "appear to diverge and contradict one another if taken at face value."[30] He continues:

Now, for any two different doctrines, it is either the case that one of them is true and the other false; or they are both false, the truth being other than either of them; or they both lead to one thing which is the truth.... That being the case...and because the manner of vision has not been ascertained, we have thought it appropriate that we direct our attention to this subject as much as we can, and seriously apply ourselves to it, and examine it, and diligently inquire into its nature.[31]

Perhaps because he began to work on *Book of Optics* while in prison, without the works of others at hand, Ibn al-Haytham does not cite earlier authorities in the book. Instead, he relies on his own observations, demonstrations, and analyses. His approach, he says, will be systematic:

We should distinguish the properties of particulars, and gather by induction what pertains to the eye when vision takes place and what is found in the manner of sensa-

Risner's *Opticae Thesaurus* starts with this image as its front page. The book included the first printed Latin translation of Al-Haytham's *Book of Optics*. The illustration incorporates many examples of optical phenomena including perspective effects, the rainbow, mirrors, and refraction.
Library of Congress registration: Alhazen, Opticae Thesvrvs, Basileae, per Episcopios, 1572.

tion to be uniform, unchanging, manifest, and not subject to doubt. After which we should ascend in our inquiry and reasonings, gradually and orderly, criticizing premises and exercising caution in regard to conclusions—our aim in all that we make subject to inspection and review being to employ justice, not to follow prejudice, and to take care in all that we judge and criticize that we seek the truth and not be swayed by opinion.[32]

To eliminate opinion and prejudice, Ibn al-Haytham supports his assertions with experimental or mathematical proofs whenever possible. Just five paragraphs after the introduction, for example, Ibn al-Haytham states that straight lines exist between "the surface of the eye" and "each point on the seen surface of the object." He continues, "An accurate experimental examination of this fact may be easily made with the help of rulers and tubes."[33]

He then describes how an observer looking through a straight tube will see only the part of an object that lies directly across from the opening of the tube. "If … he covers any part of the opening, then there will be screened off only that portion … that lies on a straight line with the eye and the screening body—this straightness being secured by the ruler and the straightness of the tube," he writes. "It follows from this experiment, with a necessity that dispels doubt, that sight does not perceive any visible object existing with it in the same atmosphere, this perception being not by reflection, except through straight lines alone that can be imagined to extend between the surface of the object and the surface of the eye."[34]

The most important discovery in *Book of Optics* appears in the very next sentence: "Sight does not perceive any visible object unless there exists in the object

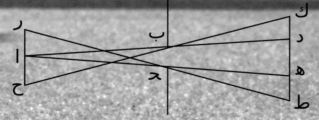

The penetration of the sun light forms the conic shape and its reverse inside the dark room. from Mustafa Nazeef Bec (1942), '*Al-Hacen Ibn Al-Haitham; his optical research and discoveries*', in Arabic, Nuri Publishing, Egypt, p.152

some light, which the object possesses of itself or which radiates upon it from another object."[35] With this simple observation, Ibn al-Haytham solved the mystery of vision that had baffled scholars for centuries. It was light, not the physical "forms" described by the physicists, that traveled from visible objects to the eye. The rays that create vision do not travel out of the eye, as the mathematicians said, but into it. Those rays are light rays.

Although Ibn al-Haytham had set out to write a book about vision, he soon realized that vision and light were inextricably linked. Consequently, a significant portion of *Book of Optics* is devoted to the study of light. Ibn al-Haytham begins by dividing light into two basic groups: primary light and secondary light. Primary light is the light radiated by an illuminating body, such as a lamp, a fire, the stars, or the sun. Secondary light is primary light that has been reflected off another surface. During the day, for example, the sun provides primary light, while every other visible object—a bird, a tree, a stone, a blade of grass—reflects the light of the sun. Even the at-

Ibn al-Haytham divides light into two basic groups: primary light and secondary light. Primary light falls from the sun to illuminate a tree branch. The secondary light then bounces off in all directions, including the direction of an observing eye.

mosphere reflects light, Ibn al-Haytham wrote, which is why the sky brightens even before the sun rises.

All light—both primary and secondary—travels in rays, originating at a single point and moving in a straight line away from that point. The light of the sun, for example, travels from a point on the sun's surface in a straight line through space. If a ray of sunlight strikes an opaque object on earth, that object will reflect it. The light reflected by an opaque object also forms a ray. It originates from a point on the surface of the object and travels away from it in a straight line.

Ibn al-Haytham states that light radiates in all directions from its source. "The light shining from a self-luminous body into the transparent air," he writes, "radiates from every part of the luminous body facing that air, ... and it issues from every point on the luminous body in every straight line that can be imagined to extend in the air from that point."[36]

To prove that light radiates in a straight line from every point of a luminous object—not just the center, the ends, or the whole—Ibn al-Haytham describes an experiment similar to the one he used to prove that visual rays travel in straight lines. He starts with a sheet of copper with a large, circular hole in the center. Through this hole, he proposes that the experimenter slide "a well-straightened cylindri-

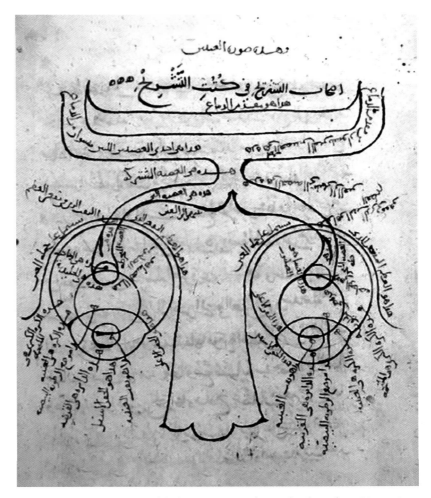

The structure of the human eye according to Ibn al-Haytham. Manuscript copy of his *Kitāb al-Manāzir* (MS Fatih 3212, vol. 1, fol. 81b, Süleymaniye Mosque Library, Istanbul)

cal tube of regular circularity and convenient length." One end of the tube is open. The other end is closed, but punctured by an aperture, which should "not exceed the thickness of a needle." The experimenter then holds a candle up to the open end of the cylinder "in the darkness of night"[37] and holds an opaque object up to the aperture at the other end. Only a small amount of the light from the flame passes through the aperture. The rest of the light is blocked by the sheet of copper.

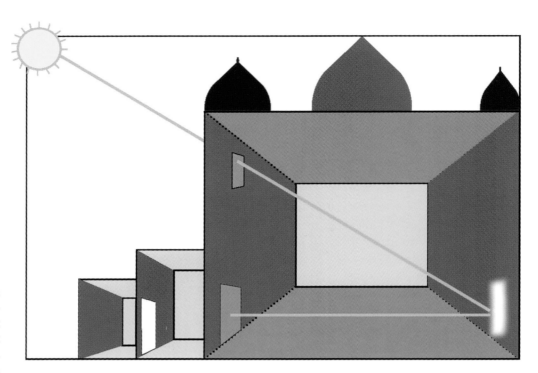

This first diagram illustrates Ibn al-Haytham's experiment that proved light radiates in all directions. The second is Ibn al-Haytham's light experiment that shows that light from several sources, when projected through a small hole, will not merge but will appear separately on the other side.

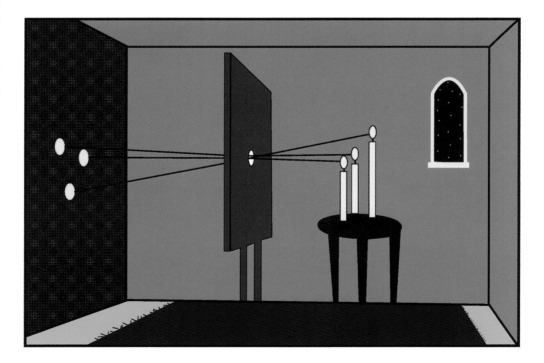

Then, he suggests, "the experimenter should ... gently move the flame so another part of it may face the hole, and then inspect the body opposite." As the flame moves, the light projected onto the opaque object changes. For example, when the tip of the flame is opposite the aperture, the light on the object appears weak. When the center of the flame is opposite the aperture, the light on the object appears bright. "Therefore," he concludes, "it appears from this experiment that light radiates from each part of the fire."[38]

What is true of primary light is also true of secondary light. "From the light that shines on any body, light radiates in every opposite direction,"[39] Ibn al-Haytham writes. This was an especially important discovery because it explains why vision remains steady even when the viewer's eye moves. According to Ibn al-Haytham's theory, a single point on any object radiates light rays into the air in all directions. If one of the rays enters the eye, it enables the viewer to see that point on the object. That same point also sends out countless rays of light that do not enter the eye. If the viewer moves his or her head slightly, the ray that originally entered the eye will miss it, but another ray, originating from the same point, will enter it. Since there are an infinite number of rays radiating from a single point, they will continue to stream into the eye as the viewer moves, providing the viewer with an uninterrupted view of that point.

Ibn al-Haytham was not content to assert that reflected light radiates in all directions; he was determined to prove it. To do so, he devised an ingenious demonstration involving darkened rooms and the light of dawn. He starts with a rectangular building with outer walls that face north, south, east, and west. The eastern wall, he writes, should have "an opening or door at the top of the wall" that allows sunlight to enter the room, striking the western wall. Directly across from the western wall is the opening to a darkened chamber. "The experimenter should observe the place when morning light shines on that wall through the opening opposite, which should be fairly wide. He will find the chamber illuminated by that light, and the light in the chamber weaker than the light on that wall. Then, as the light on the wall grows stronger, so will the light in the chamber."[40] In other words, the darkened chamber is being lit indirectly, by light reflected by the sunlit wall.

Ibn al-Haytham then proposes a second chamber positioned inside the first chamber. He finds that it, too, is illuminated. The only light entering the building comes through the opening in the eastern wall. This light illuminates the western wall, which reflects light in all directions, illuminating not only the eastern wall, but also the floor, the ceiling, and all parts of the room, including the back wall of the darkened chamber. Every illuminated point in the room, in turn, sends out light rays in all directions, so that light enters not only the darkened chamber, but also a second chamber within it. The light grows weaker each time it is reflected, but it still reaches the inner chamber.

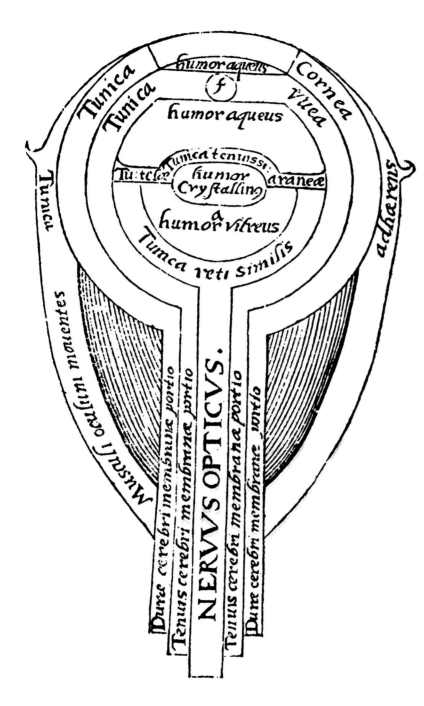

Al-Haytham's understanding of the eye, as illustrated in Risner's 1572 *Opticae thesaurus*, which included a Latin translation of *Book of Optics*.

One of Ibn al-Haytham's most important achievements was his decision to investigate the implications of his own findings. In doing so, he helped to develop what would later become known as the hypothetico-deductive method of inquiry. This method states that a possible explanation, or hypothesis, cannot be considered to be proven true unless the consequences that follow from it are also proven to be true.

Ibn al-Haytham's theory of vision suggested that light rays emanate in all directions from all illuminated objects. If this really is the case, Ibn al-Haytham deduced, each light ray must intersect, or cross, many other light rays. If intersecting light rays have any effect on each other, he reasoned, "it follows that these colors and lights will be mixed in the atmosphere and in the transparent bodies and will have reached the eye mixed; and they will affect the body of the eye while they are mixed, and thus neither the colors of the visible objects nor the objects [themselves] will be distinguished by the eye."[41] Everyday experience suggest that this does not happen. The eye can view several objects at the same time with complete clarity. Therefore, Ibn al-Haytham concluded, light rays must be able to intersect with each other without interference. Ibn al-Haytham understood that he had to prove this consequence to be true, or else his entire theory would be in doubt. To prove that light rays intersect without affecting each other, he designed what would become the most famous experiment in *Book of Optics*.

Ibn al-Haytham proposes that the experimenter position several lamps at various points in the same area, "all being opposite a single aperture leading to a dark place." On the other side of the aperture is a blank wall where the experimenter can observe the effects of the light passing through the aperture. He finds that the various lights pass through the aperture along straight paths and appear separately on the blank wall. "If one of the lamps is screened," Ibn

> **Ibn al-Haytham's theory of vision suggested that light rays emanate in all directions from all illuminated objects. If this really is the case, he deduced, each light ray must intersect, or cross, many other light rays.**

al-Haytham observes, "only the light opposite that lamp in the dark will vanish. When the screen is moved away from the lamp, that light will return to its place. Whichever lamp is screened, only the light facing it in the [dark] place will disappear. When the screen is removed, the light will return to its place."[42]

Ibn al-Haytham then proposes a variation on the same experiment, this one employing more lamps and "a chamber with a two-panel door in a dark night," which yields the same results as his original experiment. His results confirmed, Ibn al-Haytham reasons that "all the lights that appear in the dark place have reached it through the aperture alone ... therefore the lights of all those lamps have come together at the aperture, then separated after passing through it. Thus, if lights blended in the atmosphere, the lights of the lamps meeting at the aperture would have mixed in the air at the aperture and in the air preceding it before they reached the aperture, and they would have come out so mingled together that they would not be subsequently distinguishable. We do not, however, find the matter to be so; rather the lights are found to come out separately, each being opposite the lamp from which it has arrived."[43]

This experiment embodies all the elements of Ibn al-Haytham's method of inquiry. He begins by stating the problem or question: Do light rays affect each other when they intersect? Next, he gathers information by observing how light behaves in various circumstances. Based on these observations, he offers a possible answer, or hypothesis: Light rays are able to intersect without being affected by each other. He then constructs a simple experiment to test this hypothesis, forcing the lights from different lamps to cross at a single point. After repeating his experiment and confirming his results, he finds that the evidence supports his hypothesis. This systematic, step-by-step approach, based on both sound logic and observed fact,

De radiis of al-Kindi. Cambridge, Trinity College Library, Medieval manuscripts, MS R.15.17 (937). Ibn al-Haytham's lamp experiment expanded on the earlier experiments conducted by scientists like Theon of Alexandria and al-Kindi.

would come to be known as the scientific method. It is the method of inquiry that scientists around the world continue to use in various forms, to this day.

Ibn al-Haytham's lamp experiment also would gain fame because it offered the first full description of what would later become known as a camera obscura. Other scholars such as Aristotle, Theon of Alexandria, and al-Kindi had all described ways to project an image using an aperture. As a result, each has been credited with creating a kind of camera obscura. For example, Aristotle noted that sunlight traveling through small openings between the leaves of a tree, the holes of a sieve, the openings of wickerwork, and even interlaced fingers will create circular patches of light on the ground. He also noted that during a solar eclipse, these patches of light—which are actually images of the sun—will change shape. He even built a box with a small hole to let in sunlight to better observe this phenomenon.

Theon of Alexandria, a fourth-century mathematician, also experimented with small apertures, or pinholes. He observed how candlelight passing through a pinhole will create an illuminated spot on a screen that is directly in line with the aperture and the center of the candle. From this observation, which he described in his book *The Recension of the Optics* of Euclid, Theon deduced that light rays travel in straight lines. Five centuries later, al-Kindi, a ninth century Islamic philosopher, repeated Theon's candle experiment. Al-Kindi noted that not only does the light from the center of the candle's flame proceed in a straight line, but the light from each edge of the flame also proceeds in a straight line. Using a diagram, al-Kindi showed that light from the right side of the flame will pass through the aperture and end up on the left side of the screen, while light from the left side of the flame will pass through the aperture and end up on the right side of the screen.

Ibn al-Haytham knew of at least some of these experiments and no doubt was influenced by them. His lamp experiment expanded on the earlier experiments in important ways, however. For one thing, each of the earlier experiments involved only one source of light—the sun or a single candle flame. While Aristotle, Theon, and al-Kindi accurately described the effects of a single light passing through a pinhole, none of them suggests that what is being projected onto the screen is an image of everything on the other side of the aperture. By arranging several different light sources across a large area, Ibn al-Haytham leaves little doubt that an image is being projected onto the screen, even if it is only an image of lights. In the second version of his experiment, where he talks about arranging lamps outside a door, Ibn al-Haytham can be said to be describing the first camera obscura because he is projecting an image from outdoors onto a screen indoors.

As important as Ibn al-Haytham's experiments with light would prove to be, they make up only small portion of *Book of Optics*. Ibn al-Haytham divided his massive work into seven sections, or books. His experiments with lamps come from Book I, which is devoted to "the manner of vision generally."[44] In addition to descriptions of the properties of light, Book I also contains a chapter on "the structure of the eye."[45] Drawing on the work of Galen and other medical scholars, Ibn al-Haytham describes the parts of the eye in precise, even graphic detail. He correctly explains how the cornea refracts, or bends, light rays as they enter the eye. He also suggests that the optic nerve carries visual sensations to the brain.

Ibn al-Haytham was the first scientist to maintain that vision occurs in the brain, not the eyes. By doing so, he pioneered what has become known as the psychology of visual perception. He argued that personal experience affects how and what people see. For example, a small child with little experience may have a hard time interpreting things he or she sees. At the same time, an adult can make mistakes in vision because experience suggests that he or she is seeing one thing, when in reality he or she is seeing another. Ibn al-Haytham was so fascinated by errors of vision that he devoted all of Book III to the topic. Perhaps it was this awareness—that vision and perception are more subjective than most people allow—

that confirmed Ibn al-Haytham's faith in a rigorous, skeptical approach to scientific inquiry.

Like other scholars such as Archimedes and Ptolemy, Ibn al-Haytham was fascinated by the effects that flat and curved mirrors have on light. He devoted Book IV to "reflection from smooth bodies," Book V to "the forms seen inside smooth bodies," Book VI to "errors in sight in what it perceives by reflection." He also was interested in the way that transparent objects, such as water and glass, refract light. He devoted Book VII to "the manner of visual perception by refraction through transparent bodies."[46] In all four of these books, Ibn al-Haytham uses high-level geometry and mathematics to explain the behavior of light.

> **Kepler and other scientists who proved portions of *Book of Optics* wrong all did so by using the method Ibn al-Haytham pioneered—the scientific method.**

Book V contains one of the most enduring problems posed by ancient mathematics. Ibn al-Haytham imagined a scenario involving an observer, a light source, and a spherical mirror, all three in fixed locations. The observer looks upon the spherical mirror, which reflects the light from the light source. Ibn al-Haytham tried to determine the point on the spherical mirror where the light is reflected to the eye of the observer. The question had originally been formulated by Ptolemy in 150 ce, but because Ibn al-Haytham considered it extensively, it is known as "Alhazen's Problem" in the West. Ibn al-Haytham solved the problem using a geometric proof, but an algebraic solution to the problem eluded mathematicians until the end of the twentieth century.

The question had originally been formulated by Ptolemy in 150 ce, but because Ibn al-Haytham considered it extensively, it is known as Alhazen's Problem in the West. Ibn al-Haytham solved the problem using a geometric proof, and in doing so he made a major contribution to the field of mathematics that later would be known as calculus.

Ibn al-Haytham's solution to Alhazen's Problem required him to calculate the volume of a paraboloid, a curved surface that can resemble a dome, a cup, or even a Pringle potato chip. If a paraboloid intersects with a plane, the resulting intersection, known as a conic section, forms either an elliptic parabola or a hyperbolic parabola. To find the volume of a dome-shaped paraboloid, Ibn al-Haytham imagined slicing it into smaller and smaller sections. According to David Perkins, author of *Calculus and its Origins,* "Ibn al-Haytham's approach to finding a volume by cutting it into ever-thinner slices predates the official discovery of calculus in the 1600s by centuries. In fact, were ibn al-Haytham the direct ancestor of those discoverers, he would be their greatgrandfather twenty times over."[47]

Finding the volume of a paraboloid required Ibn al-Haytham to develop a formula for the sum of fourth powers of consecutive integers. The formula for the sums of squares had been stated by Archimedes around 250 bce, and the sum of cubes had been recorded by the Indian mathematician Aryabhata about 500 ce, but no one had discovered a formula for the sums of fourths. Mathematics historian Victor J. Katz observes: "The formula for the squares is not difficult to discover, and the one for cubes is virtually obvious, given some experimentation. By contrast, the formula for the sums of the fourth powers is not obvious."[48]

Ibn al-Haytham's solution is closely related to what would be called a Riemann sum in modern calculus. It was the first time a formula for sums of fourth powers had been achieved. What is even more amazing is that Ibn al-Haytham's proofs paved the way to determining the sums of other integral powers. Katz writes:

> Ibn al-Haytham showed in fact how to develop the formula for the k th pow- ers from k = 1 to k = 4; all of his proofs were similar in nature and easily gen- eralizable to the discovery and proof of formulas for the sum of any given powers of the integers.[49]

Ibn al-Haytham used his results to perform what would now be called an integration, where the formulas for the sums of integral squares and fourth powers allowed him to calculate the volume of a paraboloid. Ibn al-Haytham's formula can be written in modern notation this way:

$$\sum_{i-1}^{n} i^4 = \frac{n^5}{5} + \frac{n^4}{2} + \frac{n^3}{3} - \frac{n}{30}$$

Ibn al-Haytham's formula for the sums of fourth powers is not his only con- tribution to number theory that went uncredited for centuries. J.J. O'Connor and E.F. Robertson point out that "Ibn al-Haytham also solved problems involving congruences using what is now called Wilson's theorem: if p is prime then 1 + (p - 1) !1+(p−1)! is divisible by p."[50] Nuh Aydin, a professor of mathematics at Kenyon College, believes the theorem should be renamed. "Wilson's Theorem should really be called Alhazen's Theorem because Wilson (1741-1793) was neither the first one to state it nor to prove it. It was known by Ibn al-Haytham (but we do not have a record that he also proved it) many centuries before the European mathematicians."[51]

VI

RETURN TO BASRA

For ten long years Ibn al-Haytham remained under house arrest in Cairo. Whether he spent this time recovering from mental illness, inventing "true demonstrations relating to all objects of vision,"[52] or simply languishing in his cell is not known for certain. What is known is that on the night of February 13, 1021, Ibn al-Haytham's captor, Caliph al-Hākim Bi-amr Allah, rode his donkey into the Muqattam Hills and never returned. The Mad Caliph simply vanished. According to Al-Qiftī, government officials informed Ibn al-Haytham of this development, restored his possessions to him, and released him.

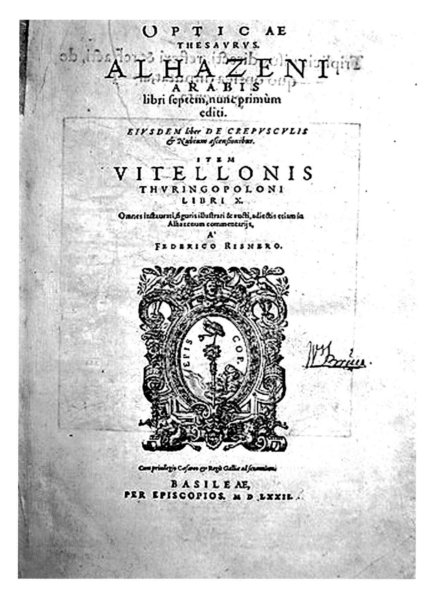

OPTICAE
THESAVRVS.
ALHAZENI
ARABIS
libri septem, nunc primùm
editi.

EIVSDEM liber DE CREPVSCVLIS
& Nubium ascensionibus.

ITEM
VITELLONIS
THVRINGOPOLONI
LIBRI X.

Omnes instaurati, figuris illustrati & aucti, adiectis etiam in
Alhazenum commentariis,

A'
FEDERICO RISNERO.

BASILEAE,
PER EPISCOPIOS. M D LXXII.

Cover page of the Latin translation of *Kitāb al-Manāzir*, or *Book of Optics*, by Ibn al-Haytham.

For the first time in ten years, Ibn al-Haytham was free to go anywhere he pleased. After years of incarceration, however, he had no money and no place to stay. Al-Qiftī reports that Ibn al-Haytham made his way to the Al-Azhar Mosque in Cairo where clerical leaders allowed him to take up residence in a domed room or tent by the gate of the mosque.

According to the twelfth-century Jewish philosopher and physician Joseph ben Judah, who lived in Cairo around 1185, Ibn al-Haytham supported himself by copying manuscripts. Joseph ben Judah told Al-Qiftī that he had heard that Ibn al-Haytham charged "the non-negotiable price"[53] of 150 silver dīnārs for making one copy each of Euclid's *Elements*, Ptolemy's *Almagest*, and the so-called *Intermediate Books*, a collection of works on astronomy and mathematics that included Euclid's *Data*, *Optics*, and *Phenomena*. Ibn al-Haytham lived on the sale of one set of these books each year, according to Joseph ben Judah. He may have also copied other books as well. The Ayasofya Library in Istanbul, Turkey, has in its collection an Arabic translation of Apollonius's *Conics* that was copied and signed by Ibn al-Haytham.

Ibn al-Haytham also appears to have been a teacher while in Cairo. Ibn Abī Usaybi'ah reports that a Fatimid scholar named al-Mubashshir ibn Fātik studied mathematics and astronomy with Ibn al-Haytham.

Usaybi'ah also states that a philosopher named Ishāq ibn Yūnus studied algebra with the Abbasid polymath.

'Ali ibn Zayd al-Bayhaqī tells an unusual story about Ibn al-Haytham's attitude towards learning. According to Al-Bayhaqī, a Syrian nobleman named Surkhab came to Ibn al-Haytham and asked if he could study with him. Ibn al-Haytham agreed to tutor the nobleman but demanded one hundred dinars a month for payment. The price was high, but Surkhab did not hesitate to pay the fee. For three years the Syrian studied with Ibn al-Haytham. At the end of this time, his education complete, Surkhab bid his tutor farewell. Ibn al-Haytham asked the nobleman to wait a moment. "You deserve this money all the more," Ibn al-Haytham said, returning all 3,600 dinars to Surkhab, "since I just wished to test your sincerity and, when I saw that for the sake of learning you cared little for money, I devoted full attention towards your education. Do remember that, in any righteous cause, it is not good to accept a return, a bribe, or a gift."[54]

Ibn al-Haytham's needs were few. According to another story told by Al-Bayhaqī, the Amir-ul-Umara of Syria offered Ibn al-Haytham a large sum of money and an annual salary to work as a scholar in his court. Ibn al-Haytham agreed to perform the service, but not at the price the Syrian leader offered. "All that I need is my daily food, a servant, and a maid to look after me," Ibn al-Haytham said. "If I amass more than the barest minimum that I need, I shall turn into your slave, and, if I spend what I save, I shall be held liable for wasting your wealth."[55]

When not teaching or copying manuscripts, Ibn al-Haytham pursued his own studies. According to three lists of Ibn al-Haytham's books that Ibn Abī Usaybi'ah included with his biography, the Abbasid scholar may have written as many as 182 treatises after his release from captivity in 1021. List I, which Usaybi'ah said he copied from a version in Ibn al-Haytham's own handwriting, covers a period up to February 10, 1027. This list contains a total of sixty-nine works—twenty-five on mathematics and forty-four on philosophy and physics. List I has no beginning date, so some of the works on it may have been written before Ibn al-Haytham was imprisoned. Others probably were written after his release.

List II, which Usaybi'ah said was also in Ibn al-Haytham's own handwriting, covers the period between February 11, 1027, to July 25, 1028. During these eighteen months Ibn al-Haytham composed another twenty-one works, including addition-

> After years of incarceration, Ibn al-Haytham made his way to the Al-Azhar Mosque in Cairo where clerical leaders allowed him to take up residence.

(Left) Ptolemy (c. 100 – c. 170), the astronomer from Alexandria of Egypt during the Roman rule, wrote several scientific treatises, which influenced Byzantine, Islamic and Western European science. *Almagest*, his treatise in astronomy, is recognized as one of the most important scientific texts of all time.

al treatises on philosophy and physics as well as works devoted to theology, medicine, optics, and astronomy. Usaybi'ah's third list contains ninety-two works—two more than Lists I and II combined. These works cover a range of topics including optics, mathematics, astronomy, music, poetry, logic, and ethics. List III is important because it is the only list of the three that contains *Book of Optics*. There is some controversy among historians over whether List III covers only the time between 1028 (the end of List II) and 1040 (the end of Ibn al-Haytham's life), or rather is a catalogue of a number of Ibn al-Haytham's works from throughout his career.

In addition to *Book of Optics*, Usaybi'ah's List III contains twelve more works on light and vision. In one of these, *Discourse on Light*, the Abbasid scholar summarizes the sections of *Book of Optics* devoted to light. Referring to *Book of Optics* by name, Ibn al-Haytham recounts the experiments with "dark chambers"[56] that show light radiates from all points of a luminous body and travels in straight lines through the air until it reaches a facing surface. In *Treatise on the Form of the Eclipse*, Ibn al-Haytham uses the camera obscura to observe "the form of the sun's [or moon's] light."[57] In doing so, he offers a correct explanation of how light traveling through an aperture becomes focused on an opaque body, such as a screen or a wall.

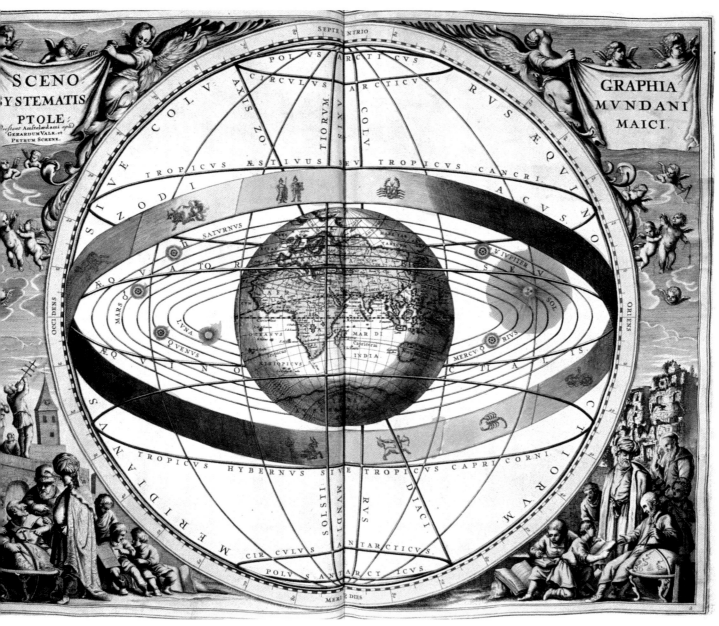

Ptolemy placed the earth at the center of his universe with the planets and stars orbiting around it. This artistic rendition comes from Andreas Cellarius's 1660 *Harmonia Macrocosmica.*

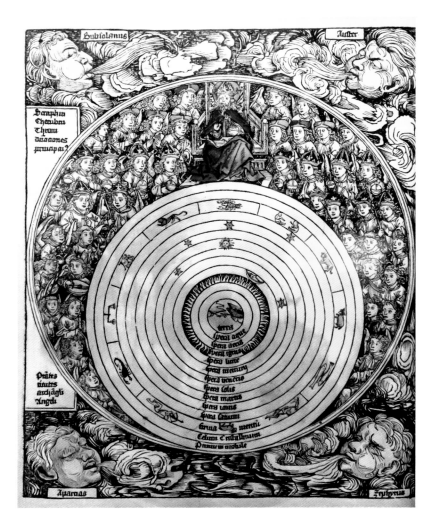

Geocentric universe and the hierarchies of cherubims and seraphims, etc., leading to God (Nuremberg Chronicle, Nuremberg, 1493. Woodcut). Hartmann Schedel's illustration from *Liber chronicarum mundi* added to al-Haytham's astronomical model, but several core components are the same. For instance, Schedel places the earth at the center with the moon, Mercury, Venus, the sun, Mars, Jupiter, and Saturn contained by the surrounding orbs.

Ibn al-Haytham's interest in refraction led him to discuss how light behaves in the atmosphere in *Treatise on the Rainbow and the Halo*. He also explored the behavior of light in astronomical works such as *Treatise on the Appearance of Stars*, *Treatise on the Lights of the Stars*, *Treatise on What Appears of the Differences in the Heights of the Stars*, and *Treatise on the Light of the Moon*. His fascination with reflection led him to write several more treatises on curved surfaces, including *Treatise on the Burning Sphere*, *Treatise on Spherical Burning Mirrors*, and *Treatise on Parabolic Burning Mirrors*.

After his release, Ibn al-Haytham finally was able to write the long-deferred commentary on Claudius Ptolemy's works. This new book, *Maqāla fī al-Shukūk 'alā Batlamyūs*, or *Doubts Concerning Ptolemy*, is Ibn al-Haytham's most important work, after *Book of Optics*. He uses his understanding of light and vision to criticize Ptolemy's discussions of optical illusions, convex mirrors, and refraction in his *Optics*. He points out contradictions between the explanations in Ptolemy's *Optics* and *Almagest* about how the atmosphere refracts the light of stars.

Ibn al-Haytham's most important criticisms involve Ptolemy's *Almagest*. He begins by noting that Ptolemy had carefully recorded "the circumstances of the heavenly bodies, their relative ordering, their distances from each other, the magnitude of their bodies, their various positions, the kinds of their motions and the varieties of their shapes." He admits that Ptolemy's records and calculations can be used to predict the positions of celestial bodies with utmost precision. However, he points out that these calculations are "based upon the motions of imaginary points on the circumferences of intellected circles."[58] Ibn al-Haytham was not satisfied with an abstract, imaginary picture of the universe. The planets and stars are real things, he argued, and any theory of their movement must take this into account. He wrote:

> Ibn al-Haytham's skepticism toward Ptolemy's model of the universe set a new standard for astronomy that required conformity to astronomical observations.

> The diameter of the epicyclic orb is an imaginary line. An imaginary line does not of its own move with a sensible motion which produces something which exists in the world. Similarly, the plane of an epicyclic orb is an imaginary plane, and an imaginary plane does not move with a sensible motion.[59]

Ptolemy had written another book, *Planetary Hypotheses*, that did offer a description of the physical configuration of the planets, but *Almagest* contradicts it. For example, to explain his observations of Mercury and Venus, Ptolemy suggests in *Almagest* that the two planets oscillate, or move back-and-forth. This explanation, Ibn al-Haytham wrote, violates common sense as well as statements in *Planetary Hypotheses* about the motion of heavenly bodies. "This is utter nonsense and contradicts his previous doctrine that the heavenly motions are equal, continuous, and unceasing,"[60] wrote Ibn al-Haytham.

What was needed, Ibn al-Haytham believed, was an explanation of how real, physical bodies move through the sky in a way that conformed to Ptolemy's observations and mathematical calculations. Ptolemy had failed to provide this. "Ptolemy assumed an arrangement that cannot exist, and the fact that this arrangement produces in his imagination the motions that belong to the planets do not free him from the error he committed in his assumed arrangement, for the existing motions of the planets cannot be the result of an arrangement that is impossible to exist,"[61] wrote Ibn al-Haytham. His skepticism toward Ptolemy's model of the universe set a new standard for astronomy. No longer would it be acceptable for astronomers to describe the movements of the heavenly bodies with imaginary points and circles. Serious astronomers would have to provide a model of the universe that conformed to astronomical observations and was consistent with the workings of nature. Ibn al-Haytham's insistence that observational data be linked to a realistic planetary scheme inspired later astronomers like Nicolaus Copernicus, Galileo Galilei, and Johannes Kepler.

The title of one of Ibn al-Haytham's later treatises offers a tantalizing clue about the last years of his life. The work is called *A Reply by [Ibn al-Haytham] to a Geometrical Question Which He Was Asked at Baghdād in the Months of the Year a.h. 418* [ce 1027-1028]. Appearing on Usaybi'ah's List II, this title indicates that Ibn al-Haytham was in Baghdad six years after the death of Caliph al-Hākim. This may not have been the first time Ibn al-Haytham had returned to his home country. A work that appears on Usaybi'ah's List I, Replies to Seven Mathematical Questions Addressed to Me in Baghdad, suggests that Ibn al-Haytham had visited the Abbasid capital before 1027 as well, although possibly while he was still living in Basra.

According to Al-Qiftī, Ibn al-Haytham spent the last twenty years of his life in Cairo and died there in 1040. Most historians accept this version of the Abbasid scholar's death and claim that his visits to Baghdad were brief. It would not have been unusual for a renowned scholar like Ibn al-Haytham to travel to different cities to meet with other scholars or participate in a *munazarah*. On the other hand, Baghdad and Cairo are about 1,400 miles (2,253 km) apart. It seems odd that Ibn al-Haytham would have made the 2,800-mile (4,506-km) journey from Cairo to Baghdad and back, not just once, but twice, around the age of sixty. His documented presence in Baghdad raises the possibility that the Abbasid scholar may have left Egypt for good, either after being released from captivity in Cairo or, as 'Ali ibn Zayd al-Bayhaqī wrote, immediately after his disastrous meeting with Caliph al-Hākim.

Another clue that Ibn al-Haytham might have lived out his old age in the Abbasid Caliphate comes from the oldest surviving manuscript of *Book of Optics*. The copyist of that manuscript was Ahmad ibn Muhammad ibn Ja'far al-'Askarī, the man who claimed in the inscription that he was Ibn al-Haytham's son-in-law. Al-'Askarī also says that he completed his copy of the manuscript in Basra. If Ibn al-Haytham died in Cairo, one has to wonder how al-'Askarī, living 1,400 miles (2,253 km) away, knew of the existence of the manuscript. Even if he did know about it, it seems highly unlikely that he would have spent several months traveling to Cairo and back to retrieve his father-in-law's book.

The date of al-'Askarī's inscription suggests that Ibn al-Haytham may not have died in Cairo. Al-'Askarī says he copied *Book of Optics* in 1082, forty-two years after Ibn al-Haytham died. If al-'Askarī's wife, Ibn al-Haytham's daughter, was born before the Abbasid scholar left for Egypt around 1010, then she would have been well into her seventies when the copy was made. In all likelihood, al-'Askarī was older than his wife. It is doubtful that al-'Askarī would have lived to be that old, let alone to have undertaken the task of copying his late father-in-law's enormous manuscript at such an advanced age.

> **Ibn al-Haytham's skepticism toward Ptolemy's model of the universe set a new standard for astronomy that required conformity to astronomical observations.**

Based on al-'Askarī's inscriptions and on Ibn al-Haytham's documented presence in the Abbasid Caliphate after 1021, it is possible that Ibn al-Haytham returned to Basra after his trip to Egypt. If he did so at age forty-six, immediately after his meeting with Caliph al-Hākim, or even at fifty-six, after being released from captivity, he certainly would have been young enough to father al-'Askarī's wife. If he was not married before he left for Egypt, he may have married for the first time when he returned. Since Muslim men were allowed to have up to four wives, Ibn al-Haytham could also have taken a second wife or married more than one woman when he returned to the Abbasid Caliphate. If Ibn al-Haytham's daughter was born after he returned to Basra, she would have been between the ages of forty and sixty when her husband copied *Book of Optics*—a much more reasonable scenario.

Whether Ibn al-Haytham spent his last years unmarried in Cairo, the scholarly hermit of legend, or married with a daughter and son-in-law in Basra, his life came to an end around 1040. According to Al-Bayhaqī, the elderly Ibn al-Haytham developed a persistent case of diarrhea. Despite intense pain, the Abbasid scholar clung to life for seven long days. Finally, feeling his life ebbing away, the man who began his career by studying religion turned towards the Kaaba, the holy shrine in Mecca that Muslims face when they pray, and recited a verse from the Qur'an: "Verily my return is to Thee; I rely upon Thee and turn unto Thee."[62] With these words, the greatest scientist of the Middle Ages left the world he had worked so hard to understand and to explain to others. Ibn al-Haytham's life was over, but the revolution he founded had scarcely begun.

"Verily my return is to Thee; I rely upon Thee and turn unto Thee."

THE KAABA AND THE QIBLA

The Kaaba is the holiest site in Islam. Muslims all around the world turn to the direction (*qibla*) of the Kaaba when they pray. According to the Qur'an, the original Kaaba was built by the ancient patriach Ibrahim and his son Ismail as a place of prayer, although many dispute this. The building has been leveled and rebuilt several times. It is located inside the Masjid al-Haram mosque in Mecca, in present-day Saudi Arabia. Built of granite and roughly cube-shaped (the word Kaaba, in Arabic, is derivative of the word "cube"), the Kaaba is traditionally covered with a gold-embroidered sheet of black silk called the *kiswah*, which is replaced annually. Surrounding the Kaaba for several miles in all directions is a restricted area known as the *haram*, covering most of Mecca, wherein only Muslims are allowed. The Kaaba forms an important part of the *hajj*, or pilgrimage to Mecca, that all solvent, able-bodied Muslims are obliged to make at least once in the course of their lifetimes. One ritual of the *hajj* is the *tawaf*, where believers circumambulate the Kaaba seven times in a counterclockwise direction.

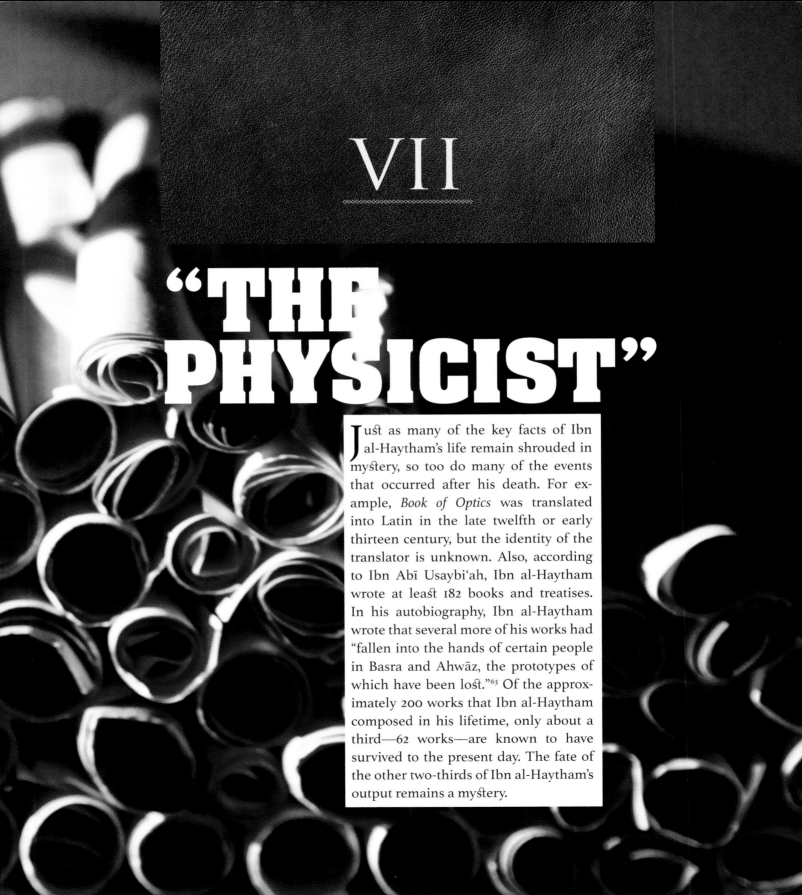

VII

"THE PHYSICIST"

Just as many of the key facts of Ibn al-Haytham's life remain shrouded in mystery, so too do many of the events that occurred after his death. For example, *Book of Optics* was translated into Latin in the late twelfth or early thirteen century, but the identity of the translator is unknown. Also, according to Ibn Abī Usaybi'ah, Ibn al-Haytham wrote at least 182 books and treatises. In his autobiography, Ibn al-Haytham wrote that several more of his works had "fallen into the hands of certain people in Basra and Ahwāz, the prototypes of which have been lost."[63] Of the approximately 200 works that Ibn al-Haytham composed in his lifetime, only about a third—62 works—are known to have survived to the present day. The fate of the other two-thirds of Ibn al-Haytham's output remains a mystery.

THE JEWISH DIASPORA

Long before the early Christians left Judea, many Jews were already living outside its border. Thousands of Jews were taken to Babylon, in what is now Iraq, to serve as slaves in 586 B.C. The Jews were allowed to return to their native land in 538 B.C., but many decided to stay behind in what became known as the first Jewish Diaspora. Over the next few centuries, trade, scholarship, and other activities drew more Jews away from their homeland. Many others were sold into slavery. In the first century B.C., Jews made up forty percent of the population of the Egyptian city of Alexandria. After Romans sacked Jerusalem in 70 A.D., many more Jews left Judea. By the end of the first century, five million Jews lived outside their homeland, outnumbering those who lived in it.

The Romans permitted the Jews a certain amount of freedom to practice their religion, but those freedoms slowly eroded under Christian rules before and after the fall of the Roman Empire. By the Middle Ages, Christians in some parts of Europe denied Jews citizenship and barred them from professional associations known as guilds. By the twelfth century, Jews in some parts of Europe were forced to live in specific sections of cities and towns, which became known as ghettos. Despite the oppression, Jews preserved their culture and religion and many excelled as scholars, philosophers, and writers.

Many of Ibn al-Haytham's missing works may have been deliberately destroyed. Even within Ibn al-Haytham's lifetime, some religious leaders looked upon some fields of learning with suspicion. We cannot know for sure, but these leaders might have misinterpreted Prophet Muhammad's saying, "May God protect us from useless knowledge."[64] According to some Islamic theologians, only knowledge that led Muslims toward God was valid. All other knowledge was excessive and potentially dangerous.

In this spirit, higher mathematics and the natural sciences were not taught within mosques when Ibn al-Haytham was himself a student. After Ibn al-Haytham's death, traditionalists began to express even greater hostility toward the subjects the Abbasid scholar had spent a lifetime exploring. "The problems of physics are of no importance for us in our religious affairs and our livelihoods," wrote the fourteenth-century historian Ibn Khaldūn. "Therefore we must leave them alone."[65] Another prominent religious leader, Ibn al-Salāh Al-Shahrazūrī, was even more peremptory. Two hundred years after Ibn al-Haytham's death, Ibn al-Salāh issued a *fatwā*, or legal opinion on Islamic law, condemning the study of philosophical sciences. "Philosophy was the foundation of foolishness," al-Salāh declared. "Logic is the introduction to philosophy, and the introduction to evil is evil."[66]

The process that led to the condemnation and censorship of Ibn al-Haytham's works did not occur everywhere at the same time. His works circulated throughout the Arabic-speaking world, into areas controlled by different sects. Attitudes toward philosophy and science varied from city to city. According to the writings of a student of Moses Maimonides, a Jewish philosopher who died in Egypt in 1204, the suppression of philosophical works was well underway in Baghdad by the beginning of the thirteenth century. The student wrote that he saw officials burn the library of a philosopher who had died in 1214. It is not known if any of Ibn al-Haytham's books or treatises were part of that philosopher's collection, but eventually some of Ibn al-Haytham's works met the same fate.

Critics of "useless knowledge" did not drive science out of Islamic society completely. Science that was useful to attaining spiritual ends continued to have a place in Muslim culture. In the thirteenth century, for example, religious leaders began to employ a person to calculate the times of the five daily prayers. The person who performed these calculations was known as the *muwaqqit*, from the Arabic word *waqt*, which means "definite time." The times of the daily prayers were traditionally linked to the movements of the sun, such as sunrise and sunset, so the *muwaqqit* had to be both an astronomer and a mathematician. Some *muwaqqit*s, such as the medieval astronomer Ibn al-Shātir, went beyond their normal duties to make new discoveries. Most, however, did not.

As the interest in pure science waned in the Islamic world, the opposite was happening in Europe. For centuries, scholars in Europe had studied only those subjects that pertained to their own religion, Christianity. Founded in the first century by Jesus of Nazareth, Christianity spread from its birthplace in Judea, a province of the Roman Empire, throughout the areas bordering the Mediterranean Sea. Suppressed for hundreds of years by leaders of the Roman Empire, Christianity eventually became the official religion of Rome in the fourth century. With the support of the Roman Empire, Christianity spread north through Europe and east through Asia Minor.

Like the Muslims, the Christians believed that the purpose of earthly life was to live according to God's revealed laws and teachings. As in the Islamic world, most education in Christendom took place in the churches and centered on religious thought. Christianity's greatest thinkers were theologians and philos-

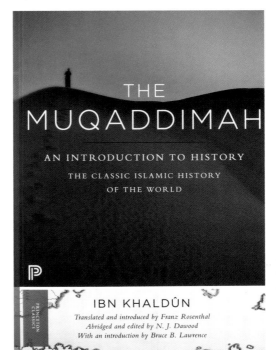

The Muqaddimah is the masterpiece of Ibn Khaldun, a fourteenth century historian, who is considered as the founder of sociology.

Moses Maimonides (d. 1204) was a Rabbi and one of the leading philosophers of the Middle Ages.

Alhambra Palace, Granada, Spain. The seat of the Muslim rule in Spain until 1492 and now a UNESCO World Heritage Site, the Alhambra features qualities of Muslim, Christian, and Jewish art.

ophers. By the twelfth century, however, Christian scholars were beginning to broaden their interests into other areas, including the realm of science.

The only area of medieval Europe that had eluded the grasp of Christendom was al-Andalus, located on the Iberian peninsula, which remained under Muslim rule. Like Muslims throughout the world, the rulers of al-Andalus believed that Jews and Christians were both *Ahl al-Kitab*, or "People of the Book." According to Islamic theology, non-Muslims who revered sacred books, such as the Jewish Torah and the Christian Bible, were different from other non-Muslims, who were considered nonbelievers or heathens.

The Muslims believed that the ancient Jewish prophets were divinely inspired and that the books that told of their revelations were holy. "We believe in Allah and that which is revealed unto us and that which was revealed unto Abraham and Ishmael and Isaac and Jacob and the tribes, and that which was vouchsafed unto Moses and Jesus and the prophets from their Lord. We make no distinction between any of them, and to Him we have surrendered,"[67] reads a verse of the Qur'an. Because of their closeness to God, People of the Book were not required to convert to Islam, and Muslim leaders were bound by faith not to interfere with their worship. "He who wrongs a Jew or a Christian will have myself as his indicter on the day of judgment,"[68] Prophet Muhammad declared.

Gardens of
Cordoba

Although relations between Andalusian Muslims, Christians, and Jews were by no means always peaceful, a general atmosphere of tolerance prevailed, making al-Andalus a vibrant center of learning. In Toledo, Córdoba, and other Andalusian cities, Muslim, Jewish, and Christian scholars exchanged views and shared information. Through the Muslims, Jewish and Christian scholars came into contact with the works of the ancient Greeks, which had been preserved in Arabic translations. They also discovered the works of Islamic scholars such as al-Khwarizmi, Ibn al-Kindi, and Ibn al-Haytham.

Word of the Islamic libraries gradually spread beyond the borders of al-Andalus. In the twelfth century, for example, an Italian named Gerard of Cremona wanted to read Ptolemy's *Almagest*, an often-praised but little-read book that had not been available in a Latin translation for centuries. Gerard heard, however, that an Arabic translation of the Greek astronomer's book was available in the Andalusian city of Toledo. Gerard traveled to Toledo, learned Arabic, and read the book.

Once in Toledo, Gerard discovered works by other Greeks that also had been translated into Arabic. Rather than returning to Italy, Gerard stayed in al-Andalus and began translating Arabic books into Latin. In addition to *Almagest*, Gerard translated books by Aristotle, Euclid, and Galen. Gerard soon found that Islamic scholars had not only preserved the works of the ancient Greeks, but they had commented on them, expanded on them, and even surpassed them with their discoveries. He began to translate books by Islamic scholars such as the Iranian physician Abu 'Ali al-Husayn ibn 'Abd Allah ibn Sina, known in Latin as Avicenna.

As Gerard of Cremona began to grasp the extent of Islamic knowledge, he realized that he could not translate all of the important Arabic books by himself. He began to recruit other scholars to help translate the treasures of Islamic learning. Just as Caliph al-Ma'mun had founded the House of Wisdom in Baghdad four hundred

Medieval European scholars were impressed with *De aspectibus*' novel ideas about vision, its detailed account of the anatomy of the eye, and its description of experiments that any person could duplicate.

years earlier to translate the works of the Greeks, Gerard of Cremona founded a center in Toledo to translate the works of Islamic scholars. In all, Gerard and his followers translated more than eighty Arabic works into Latin. One of those works was *On Paraboloidal Burning Mirrors* by Ibn al-Haytham.

Many of the twelfth- and thirteenth-century European translators working in Gerard's center did not sign their manuscripts. Such was the case of the translator who came across a massive Arabic text entitled *Kitāb al-Manāzir*. The anonymous scholar translated the title of this work simply as *De aspectibus*, or *The Optics*. He called the author Alhacen, a Latinized form of al-Hasan. *De aspectibus* fascinated medieval European scholars. They were impressed with its novel ideas about vision, its detailed account of the anatomy of the eye, and its description of experiments that any person could duplicate. It became one of the most copied works of medieval Islamic science. The Latin translation of *Kitāb al-Manāzir* is far from perfect. Rather than quoting Ibn al-Haytham, the translator often paraphrases him. Because of the translator's lack of knowledge about optics, the paraphrased sections can be misleading. The translator also condensed the book by leaving out whole passages. For example, the translator includes the camera obscura experiment in Book I, Chapter 6, that involves a screen, but he leaves out the following experiment with the two-panel door. Perhaps most grievously, he also omits the first three chapters of Book I.

Whether the Latin translator skipped the first three chapters, or the Arabic manuscript he possessed did not contain them in the first place, the readers of *De aspectibus* missed out on vital information. Ibn al-Haytham's description of the two earlier theories of vision; initial observations and conclusions about the nature and properties of light; elegant thoughts on the difficulty of achieving certainty in matters of science; his entire method of inquiry—all these important points were left out.

Because of these omissions, European scholars were not able to fully understand Ibn al-Haytham's theories of light, especially his description of how it radiates from primary and secondary sources. Without this basic information, European scholars often appended their own theories to support those of Ibn al-Haytham. Unfortunately, some scholars used popular ideas about how living creatures multiply to explain the propagation of light. The inclusion of these apocryphal explanations in *De aspectibus* caused confusion for years to come.

Even without the first three chapters, however, many of Ibn al-Haytham's revolutionary ideas came through to European readers. Because he often alludes to earlier portions of his book, some of the observations and conclusions contained in the first three chapters of Book I are mentioned later. Ibn al-Haytham's method, although not explicitly spelled out in the original Latin translation, is evident throughout the book.

One of the first medieval scholars to read and respond to Ibn al-Haytham's masterpiece was a Franciscan monk named Roger Bacon. Born in a prosperous family around 1220 in England, Bacon may well have been schooled in Latin and arithmetic by a local priest. He enrolled in the University of Oxford at the age of thirteen—the common age to start a university education at that time. After receiving a master of arts degree from Oxford and briefly joining the faculty of the university, Bacon moved to Paris in 1241 and remained there for six years, lecturing on Aristotle at the University of Paris. There he met Peter Peregrinus of Maricourt, the author of the earliest known treatise on magnets and magnetism. This meeting appears to have changed not only the course of Bacon's life, but the history of science in Europe as well.

Bacon returned to Oxford and devoted himself to the study of optics, astronomy, mathematics, and alchemy—a chemical science and speculative philosophy that aimed to transform common metals into gold—as well as to discover a universal cure for disease and a way to prolong life indefinitely. One of the books in Bacon's collection appears to have been *De aspectibus*. Bacon referred to Alhazen by name and discussed his work in Book Five of his *Opus Majus*, or *Greater Work*.

Bacon accepted Ibn al-Haytham's theories about light and repeated some of his experiments, including the one with the camera obscura. Most importantly, Bacon endorsed the Abbasid scholar's method of inquiry. Throughout his writings, Bacon stressed the importance of experimentation in the discovery of scientific truth. Throughout Europe during Bacon's time, a movement called Scholasticism was gaining strength. Aiming to reconcile classical knowledge with Christian theology, Scholasticism based its teachings largely on consultation with authorities like Aristotle and the Church. Although he admired Aristotle, Bacon believed that knowledge should be pursued independently, without the influence of previously maintained dogmas. Bacon may have taken his cues from Ibn al-Haytham, who also revered Aristotle but wrote *Book of Optics* without reference to other thinkers, establishing all of his conclusions on the basis of experimentation, observation, mathematics, and deduction.

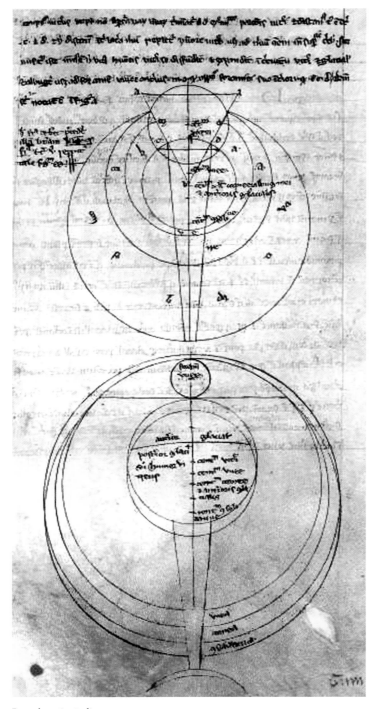

Bacon's optic studies

Although Bacon acknowledged his debt to Ibn al-Haytham in the field of optics, he did not give the Arab scholar credit for having developed the method of inquiry that he so strongly advanced. Instead, Bacon praised Peter Peregrinus as the *dominus experimentorum,* or the master of experiments. "[Peregrinus] gains knowledge of matters of nature, medicine, and alchemy through experiment," Bacon wrote, "and all that is in the heaven and in the earth beneath."[69]

Bacon may have credited Peregrinus over Ibn al-Haytham for pioneering the experimental method because he knew the Frenchman personally and revered his work. He may have had another motive. Bacon and Peregrinus were devout Christians at a time when Christians and Muslims were fighting for control of Jerusalem and the areas around it in a series of wars known as the Crusades. Bacon was a member of the clergy and Peregrinus had even fought in one of the Crusades himself. Because of these ongoing conflicts, Bacon may have felt that attaching an Islamic scholar's name to the scientific method would slow its acceptance among Christians.

Another Franciscan friar deeply impressed with *De aspectibus* was John Pecham. Ten years younger than Bacon, Pecham was born in Sussex, England, around 1230 and educated at the University of Paris. He was so inspired by *De aspectibus* that he decided to summarize it, much as Ibn al-Haytham had once summarized the works of Ptolemy and Euclid. Pecham patterned his book, *Perspectiva communis,* after

Bacon accepted Ibn al-Haytham's theories about light and repeated some of his experiments, including the one with the camera obscura.

De aspectibus, and he frequently references Ibn al-Haytham, whom he calls "the Author' or "the Physicist."

While Pecham was condensing Ibn al-Haytham's work, another European scholar was expanding on it. Erazmus Ciolek Witelo, also known as Witelo, was a friar of the Roman Catholic church who attended college in the Italian city of Padua around 1260. He later traveled to the Italian city of Viterbo where he met William of Moerbeke, a renowned translator of Aristotle. At some point, Witelo came across *De aspectibus.* Like Bacon and Pecham, Witelo was impressed with Ibn al-Haytham's work. He decided to write his own book on optics, which he called *Perspectiva* and dedicated to William of Moerbeke. Although Witelo does not cite Ibn al-Haytham by name, the structure of his *Perspectiva* is identical to the organization of *De aspectibus.* The content is similar as well. Through Bacon, Pecham, and Witelo, Ibn al-Haytham's ideas and methods spread through Europe.

Roger Bacon

109

Scholars continued to read Ibn al-Haytham's work independently of his European commentators, as well. At the beginning of the fourteenth century, *De aspectibus* was translated from Latin—the language of scholars—into Italian, the common language of the Italian people. This translation made Ibn al-Haytham's discoveries available to people in trades and business. One of those who studied *Book of Optics* was the Italian sculptor Lorenzo Ghiberti.

Born in 1378 in the town of Pelago, outside Florence, Ghiberti gained fame as the sculptor of a pair of doors for the cathedral of Florence. The figures that Ghiberti sculpted on these doors were rendered in a flat and angular style. Around 1425, however, Ghiberti's style changed. "Following the completion of the first doors, Ghiberti embarked on a decade of intense exploration of new ways of forming pictorial space and making gracefully active and lifelike figures," writes Constance Lowenthal, Executive Director of the International Foundation for Art Research in New York City. "His works of the late 1420s show him able to make space increasingly intelligible in a series of clearly receding planes; using shallow relief, Ghiberti depicted volumes of bodies and deep architectural spaces."[70]

Ghiberti was not the only artist to suddenly figure out how to create the illusion of three-dimensional space on a flat surface. All across Europe, artists began to create realistic perspective in paintings, drawings, and shallow relief sculptures.

The Italian sculptor Lorenzo Ghiberti, known for a pair of magnificent doors he sculpted for the baptistery of the Florence Cathedral, reported having read *Book of Optics*.

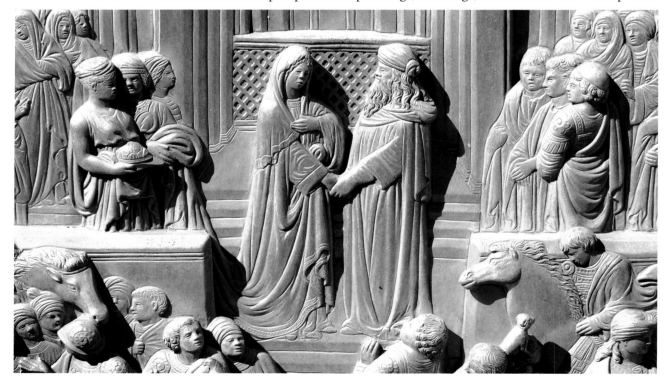

The people and animals in these works seemed more solid and alive than those in earlier works. The artists also began reproduce elaborate details, such as the lace on clothing and tablecloths, with photographic realism.

In his book *Secret Knowledge*, the renowned British artist David Hockney suggests that this sudden change occurred because artists began using the camera obscura to project three-dimensional scenes onto flat surfaces and trace the images. "I'm suggesting that artists saw these projections. They're very simple to make, and when you make them, they're very beautiful and exciting," Hockney told Leslie Stahl of CBS News. "It's hard to believe that in the 15th century they would say, 'What an amusing novelty, how interesting ...but let's not use that,'" he says. Hockney sets the date for this change at about the same time Ghiberti began to study perspective. "We did come to about 1420, and realized something happens,"[71] he says.

Historians know for certain that the Italian artist Leonardo da Vinci was familiar with the camera obscura, because he wrote about it in his notebooks. "When the images of illuminated objects pass through a small round hole into a very dark room...you will see on the paper all those objects in their natural shapes and colors," Leonardo wrote around 1510. "They will be reduced in size, and upside down, owing to the intersection of the rays at the aperture."[72]

> **Historians know for certain that the Italian artist Leonardo da Vinci was familiar with the camera obscura, because he wrote about it in his notebooks.**

Leonardo and other artists learned that they could place glass lenses near the aperture of the camera obscura to better focus and project the image. Hockney points to the softness in some of Leonardo's paintings, such as "Mona Lisa," as evidence that he used the camera obscura in his work. "Leonardo describes the camera obscura, meaning he tried it out and looked at the pictures," Hockney said. "Whether he used the lens for ["Mona Lisa"] I don't know. He wouldn't need it, but he'd already seen the wonderful softness."[73]

Some art historians dispute Hockney's contentions. They suggest that other factors are responsible for the sudden change in European art. "Isn't there something about those cultures, the fact that they're predominantly urban, mercantile, sophisticated, with a strong middle class," asks Walter Liedtke, curator of European paintings at New York's Metropolitan Museum of Art. Hockney rejects this explanation. "All these art historians, not one of them ever took the trouble to look through a camera obscura to see what it was like,"[74] Hockney responds.

Art historian Francesca Fiorani believes that Ibn al-Haytham influenced Leonardo in a much more fundamental way than simply by introducing him to a mechanical device for limning the outlines of objects and locating the details on those objects—the folds of a fabric or the pupils of a person's eyes. Fiorani argues that Ibn al-Haytham's analysis of all questions relating to light and vision provided Leonardo with a scientific foundation for understanding how marks of paint on a panel or wall might perceived by a viewer. She points out that Leonardo's "shadow drawings," which depict light from a candle striking a ball, reveal his understanding of Ibn al-Haytham's ideas about how each individual light ray emanates from one point and strikes another—the point-to-point propagation of light. "Depicting the light not as we see it—as one solid beam—but rather as a set of discrete rays, he charted the individual destination of each and every one, line by line. Clearly, he knew something about the science of optics—or at least how light behaves when it hits an opaque object," [75] she writes.

Fiorani then asks the important question: "If optics informed Leonardo's art almost from the start, how might he have acquired this knowledge?" She notes that books exploring the science of optics were available in Latin, but that was a language Leonardo "never mastered." However, she continues: "There was an eleventh-century manuscript titled *Book of Optics* by the Arab philosopher known in the Renaissance as Alhacen—his real name was Abu Ali al-Hasan Ibn al-Haytham—that Renaissance artists knew about, because it had been translated into the vernacular. A copy of this Italian translation was in the hands of an artist Leonardo knew." [76]

Fiorani believes that certain passages in Leonardo's notebooks suggest that the artist was intimately familiar with the Italian translation of *Book of Optics*. She writes:

> We know that Leonardo would take notes whenever he read a book. Not surprisingly, written on scraps of paper and in his notebooks are thoughts that are so deeply aligned with Alhacen's book that they seem, at times, nearly direct quotes from it—such as Alhacen's belief in the truthfulness of sensory experience.... Even the way Leonardo described painting—as an activity that "embraces all the ten functions of the eye; that is to say darkness, light, body and color, shape and location, distance and closeness, motion and rest"—is a rephrasing of Alhacen's description of the eight conditions that make proper human vision possible: "distance between eye and object, a facing orientation, light, size, opacity, transparency in the air, time, and a healthy eye." [77]

Leonardo's knowledge of the science behind light, shadow, color, and reflection allowed him to not only depict objects realistically, but also to capture nuances of people's expressions that reveal what they might be thinking and how they might be feeling. "By paying attention to these shadows, an artist with some knowledge of optics could work backward from the interplay of light and dark to more accurately render the human form—and to better convey the emotions it expressed," writes Fiorani. It was this ability that sets Leonardo's work apart from others and

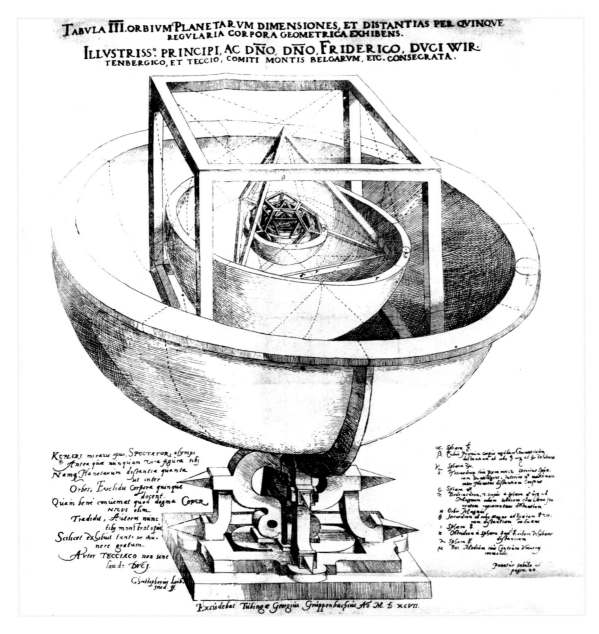

Kepler's explanation of the structure of the planetary system. Johannes Kepler was among the seventeenth-century scholars who referred to Alhazen (Ibn al-Haytham) by name in their works.

113

continues to make it relevant to modern viewers. "For Leonardo, the focus was on the inner emotional lives of the people he portrayed, including how they reacted in the face of the divine,"[78] writes Fiorani. "It was his emphasis on the human, on how human beings instinctually react to others and to the world, that gives his paintings such a modern feel, that allows them to continue to speak to us even after five hundred years."[79]

As *Book of Optics* was revolutionizing European art, it also was gaining notoriety in the academic community. In 1572 a Swiss publisher named Frederick Risner published *De aspectibus* and Witelo's *Perspectiva* together in one book called *Opticae thesaurus*. The two earlier books were so similar that Risner used several of same illustrations for both texts and included many cross-references between them. Through Risner, thousands of scholars and students across Europe became familiar with Ibn al-Haytham's methods and ideas.

By the time Risner published the *Opticae thesaurus,* Europe was in the middle of a period of discovery and learning known as the Renaissance. Scholars in many fields made tremendous advances. For example, in 1543 the Polish astronomer Nicolaus Copernicus proposed the theory that the earth rotated on its own axis every twenty-four hours and that it and the other planets revolved around the sun. In 1572, the same year Risner published Ibn al-Haytham's work, the Danish astronomer Tycho Brahe observed the birth of a new star in the constellation Cassiopeia, a finding that challenged the widespread belief that the stars were permanently fixed in the sky. In 1610, the Italian mathematician and astronomer Galileo Galilei used the newly invented telescope to discover four moons revolving around Jupiter—a discovery that helped confirm the Copernican model of orbiting planets and moons. Galileo also used mathematics and experimentation to prove wrong many of Aristotle's theories about motion. He was another prominent spokesman of experimental science.

As learning in Europe increased, so did the appreciation and recognition of Ibn al-Haytham. For the first time, Europeans had the skills to fully appreciate the higher mathematics contained in *Book of Optics*. Seventeenth-century mathematicians such as Pierre de Fermat of France, Thomas Harriot of England, Isaac Beeckman and Willebrord van Roijen Snell of the Netherlands, and Johannes Kepler of Germany all referred to Alhazen by name in their works.

Kepler used Ibn al-Haytham's own methods to disprove one of the Abbasid scholar's theories about vision. Kepler filled a glass sphere with water to represent an eye filled with fluids. He then placed the glass sphere near the aperture of a camera obscura and observed the result. He found that the rays entering through the aperture were bent by the glass and the fluid in a way that created a *"pictura"* or image—upside down and backwards—on the back of the sphere. This experi-

In the frontispiece to Hevelius's *Selenographia*, Ibn al-Haytham represents Ratione (the use of reason) with his geometrical proof and Galileo represents Sensu (the use of the senses) with his telescope. The two scientists hold the book's title page between them, suggesting a harmony between the methods.

When Napoleon Bonaparte occupied Egypt in 1798, Islamic scholars began to fully appreciate how far behind the Europeans they had fallen.

ment led Kepler to conclude that the eye works like a camera obscura, with the pupil serving as an aperture and the retina as the receiving screen. The optic nerve carries the image from the retina to the brain, which inverts the image so that it perceives object right side up.

For more than six hundred years—two hundred years longer than the period from Galileo's death to today—Ibn al-Haytham had reigned as the world's leading authority in several fields. By the middle of the seventeenth century, however, European scientists had refined, expanded on, and surpassed most of his discoveries. In 1637, for example, the French scientist and mathematician René Descartes, who had read *Book of Optics*, published three essays—*Dioptrics*, *Meteorology*, and *Geometry*—that expanded on Ibn al-Haytham's discoveries regarding refraction, the rainbow, and analytic geometry. The Dutch physicist Christian Huygens also read Ibn al-Haytham's masterpiece and answered many of its unsolved questions.

Although no longer hailed as "the Physicist," Ibn al-Haytham still was revered as one of the founders of modern science. When the Polish astronomer Johannes Hevelius published an atlas of the moon in 1647, the frontispiece bore the likenesses of the two pillars of experimental science up to that time: Galileo, shown holding a telescope, and Ibn al-Haytham, depicted with a geometric drawing in his hand.

Four years after Hevelius honored Ibn al-Haytham on the frontispiece of his lunar atlas, another scientist went a step further: He put the Abbasid scholar's name on a map of the moon. In 1651, a Jesuit priest named Gianbattista Riccioli published a book entitled *Almagestum Novum* that included new maps of the lunar surface. Riccioli began the tradition of naming craters after scientists and other scholars. He named one of most prominent craters for Copernicus, and two others for Galileo and Kepler. He reserved some sections of his map for ancient Greeks, some for ancient Romans, some for his contemporaries, and some for medieval and Arabic scholars. About fifteen degrees north of the Moon's equator, just to the east of Mare Crisium, stands a circular impact crater about 30 kilometers wide. Riccioli named this crater Alhazen. In 1935 the International Astronomical Union (IAU), the internationally recognized authority for naming celestial bodies and their surface features, standardized the names of six hundred lunar features, including the crater Riccioli named for Ibn al-Haytham.

With the passage of time, Ibn al-Haytham's name and achievements faded into history, but around the beginning of the twentieth century things began to change. Scholars such as Carl Brockelmann, Heinrich

As part of the International Year of Light and Light-based Technologies, UNESCO launched a series of interactive exhibits and workshops depicting the life and work of Ibn al-Haytham.

Suter, and Eilhard Wiedemann—all from Germany—traveled to Istanbul and other centers of Islamic learning and unearthed long-forgotten works by the Abbasid scholar. In 1936, Max Krause, another German scholar, published a list of manuscript copies of *Kitāb al-Manāzir* that included a reference to the manuscript that had been copied by Ibn al-Haytham's son-in-law, ibn Ja'far al-'Askarī. Since then, scholars have translated the complete *Kitāb al-Manāzir*—including the three chapters missing from the Latin translation—into the major European languages. Many of his other works, including *Doubts Concerning Ptolemy* and *Completion of the Conics of Apollonius* also have been translated into Western languages. For the first time in centuries, scholars began to appreciate the breadth of Ibn al-Haytham's knowledge.

Ibn al-Haytham's reputation rose in the Arab world as well. When French troops under the leadership of Napoleon Bonaparte occupied Egypt in 1798, Islamic scholars began to fully appreciate how far behind the

Europeans they had fallen. "Our country must change its ways, and new sciences must be introduced,"[80] declared Sheik Hassan al-ʿAttār, after examining the technology the French brought to Cairo. When the Ottoman leader Muhammad ʿAli became the viceroy of Egypt in 1805, he began to modernize Egyptian education. In 1836 ʿAli proposed an educational mission to France to gather information about modern military technology, engineering, medicine, physical science, and mathematics. Sheik ʿAttār, then rector of the Al-Azhar Mosque, recommended his former pupil, Rifāʿa Rāfi al-Tahtāwī, to lead the mission. Upon his return from Europe, al-Tahtāwī became the director of the School of Languages, an institution devoted the translation and study of scientific works. As Muslim students and teachers absorbed the lessons of Europe, they came to appreciate the role Islamic scholars such as Ibn al-Haytham had played in the scientific revolution of the Renaissance.

As the millennial anniversary of Ibn al-Haytham's birth approached, scholars around the world prepared to honor one of the foremost founders of modern science. The nation of Pakistan issued a special stamp commemorating Ibn al-Haytham as the "Father of Optics." In 1969 the Hamdard National Foundation, a charitable organization founded with proceeds from the Hamdard medical laboratories, sponsored a celebration of the one-thousandth anniversary of Ibn al-Haytham's birth. Scientists and historians traveled to the University of Karachi, in Karachi, Pakistan, to deliver papers and discuss the Abbasid scholar's legacy.

Their scientific heritage reclaimed and renewed, Muslims around the world celebrated the memory of Ibn al-Haytham in public life. In 1971 the nation of Qatar issued a postage stamp honoring Ibn al-Haytham as part of the "Famous Men of Islam" series. Leaders in the Hashemite Kingdom of Jordan named a hospital in Amman after the Abbasid scholar. Not far from where Ibn al-Haytham took part in *munazarah* stands the Ibn al-Haytham College of Education, part of the University of Baghdad. Children in central Baghdad attend Ibn al-Haytham Elementary School, while boys in the Palestinian city of Nablus attend the Ibn al-Haytham Elementary School for Boys. On April 4, 1992, Saddam Hussein, the former leader of Iraq, established the Ibn Al Haytham Missile Research and Design Center, dedicated to the development of ballistic missiles.

Ibn al-Haytham has been featured on Iraqi currency at various times in history. In 1931 the government of Iraq began issuing a new banknote, the dinar, to replace the Indian rupee as the official currency of Iraq. The new banknotes featured images of Iraqi landmarks and historical figures, including Ibn al-Haytham. After the first Persian Gulf War in 1991, the government of Iraq issued new currency. A portrait of Saddam Hussein replaced the image of Ibn al-Haytham on the 10-dinar note. After a coalition of forces led by the United States deposed Saddam Hussein in 2003, the Iraqis formed a new government. On October 15, 2003, the Central Bank of Iraq issued new currency based on the old banknote designs. The Central Bank decided to decorate the face of the new 10,000-dinar note—the second-largest denomination in the new currency—with a portrait of Ibn al-Haytham, Iraq's greatest scientist, as a symbol of progress and achievement for the new nation.

In 2013 the United Nations General Assembly designated 2015 as the International Year of Light and Light-based Technologies. As part of the celebration, the United Nations Educational, Scientific and Cultural Organization (UNESCO) teamed up with the cultural heritage organization 1001 Inventions to launch a series of interactive exhibits, workshops and live shows depicting the life and work of Ibn al-Haytham. "I am pleased to partner with the International Organization 1001 Inventions to launch the World of Ibn Al Haytham Global Campaign, to promote light-science for the benefit of all," said UNESCO Director-General Irina Bokova, announcing the program. "The life and work of Ibn Al-Haytham have never been as relevant as they are today."[81] International Year of Light and Light-based Technologies (IYL2015) Chairman John Dudley added, "Ibn Al-Haytham was a remarkable pioneer known for his insistence on understanding our world through experimental verification, and it will be a pleasure to work throughout 2015 to make his story known worldwide."[82]

Were he alive today, Ibn al-Haytham no doubt would applaud the goals and aspirations of modern science, but he would have cautioned students and scholars everywhere to regard all sources of information, including his own works, with a healthy skepticism. "Truth is sought for itself, but the truths are immersed in uncertainties, and authorities are not immune from error, nor is human nature itself," he wrote in *Doubts Concerning Ptolemy*. He continued:

> The seeker after truth is not one who studies the writings of the ancients and, following his natural disposition, puts his trust in them, but rather the one who suspects his faith in them and questions what he gathers from them, the one who submits to argument and demonstration, and not to the sayings of a human being whose nature is fraught with all kinds of imperfection and deficiency. Thus, the job of the man who investigates the writings of scientists, if learning the truth is his goal, is to make himself an enemy of all that he reads, and applying his mind to the core and margins of its content, attack it from every side. He should also suspect himself as he performs his critical examination of it, so that he may avoid falling into either prejudice or leniency.[83]

TIMELINE

965
Abū ʿAlī al-Hasan ibn al-Hasan ibn al-Haytham is born in Basra, in what was then the Abbasid Caliphate and is now the Republic of Iraq.

circa 975
Attends school in the local mosque.

c. 985
Begins theological studies in earnest.

c. 990
Abandons theology; discovers the works of Aristotle.

c. 995
Studies and begins to write commentaries on the work of Greek mathematicians.

c. 1000
Appointed to a government post in Basra; writes books on practical subjects such as measurement, the construction of water clocks, and astronomy; suggests a plan to dam the Nile.

c. 1005
Shows signs of mental illness; relieved from government post.

1010
Receives summons from Fatimid Caliph al-Hakim.

1011
Travels to Egypt and meets Caliph al-Hakim; according to one account, travels to Aswan and assesses the feasibility of building a dam on the Nile; reports his findings to al-Hakim in Cairo; admits failure; is given a government post; shows signs of mental illness; is placed under house arrest.

1011-1021
Living in isolation under house arrest, probably composes some or all of *Book of Optics*.

1021
Death of Caliph al-Hakim; released from house arrest; begins writing new books and treatises.

1027
Writes an autobiographical sketch.

c. 1027
Travels to Baghdad and participates in a *munazarah*.

1028-1040
Composes as many as ninety-two new works, including twelve about light and vision.

c. 1040
Dies after a persistent case of diarrhea.

NOTES

CHAPTER ONE: Boyhood in Basra

1. Ibn al-Haytham, *The Optics of Ibn al-Haytham*, tr. A.I. Sabra. London: The Warburg Institute, 1989, pp. 3-4.
2. Ibid. p. 3.
3. The Qur'an, The Family of Imran, verse 191.
4. Quoted in "Ten Misconceptions about Islam," USC-MSA Compendium of Muslim Texts, http://www.usc.edu/dept/MSA/notislam/misconceptions.html.
5. Quoted in "Thousand and One Nights, The." Encyclopædia Britannica. 2005. Encyclopædia Britannica Premium Service. 4 Aug. 2005, http://www.britannica.com/eb/article-9072265.

CHAPTER TWO: The Quest for Knowledge

6. Quoted in Dr. Naseer Ahmad Nasir, "Ibn al-Haitham and His Philosophy." *Ibn al-Haitham, Proceedings of the Celebrations of 1000th Anniversary*, Hakim Mohammed Said, ed. Sadar, Pakistan: The Times Press, 1969, p. 82.
7. Ibid.
8. Ibid.
9. Islam. (2005). *Encyclopædia Britannica*. Retrieved August 25, 2005, from Encyclopædia Britannica Premium Service http://www.britannica.com/eb/article-69166
10. Quoted in Dr. Naseer Ahmad Nasir, p. 82.
11. Ibid.
12. Ibid.
13. Ibid.
14. Ibid.
15. Quoted in Saleh Beshara Omar, *Ibn al-Hyatham's* Optics. Minneapolis: Bibliotheca Islamica, 1977, p.13.
16. Quoted in Dr. Naseer Ahmad Nasir, p. 82.
17. Ibid.
18. Ibid.
19. Ibid. p. 88.
20. Ibid. p. 86-87.
21. Ibid. p. 86.

CHAPTER THREE: "Madness"

22. Abdul Ghafur Chaudhri, "Ibn al-Haitham: The Educational and Scientific Importance of his Writings." *Ibn al-Haitham, Proceedings of the Celebrations of 1000th Anniversary*, Hakim Mohammed Said, ed. Sadar, Pakistan: The Times Press, 1969, p. 116.
23. Quoted in Dr. Naseer Ahmad Nasir, p. 93.
24. Quoted in Serajul Haque, Ph. D., "A Peep into the Life and Works of Ibn al-Haitham." *Ibn al-Haitham, Proceedings of the Celebrations of 1000th Anniversary*, Hakim Mohammed Said,
ed. Sadar, Pakistan: The Times Press, 1969, p. 171.
25. Quoted in Dr. Naseer Ahmad Nasir, p. 82.

CHAPTER FOUR: To Egypt!

26. Quoted in Dr. Naseer Ahmad Nasir, p. 93.
27. Ibid.
28. Quoted in Ibn al-Haytham, *The Optics of Ibn al-Haytham*, tr. A.I. Sabra. London: The Warburg Institute, 1989, vol. II, p. xix.

CHAPTER FIVE: The Scholar of Cairo

29. Ibid. Vol. I, p. 6.
30. Ibid. Vol. I, p. 4.
31. Ibid. Vol. I, p. 5.
32. Ibid. Vol. I, pp. 5-6.
33. Ibid. Vol. I, p. 7.
34. Ibid. Vol. I, p. 8.
35. Ibid.
36. Ibid. Vol. I, p. 20.
37. Ibid. Vol. I, p. 18.
38. Ibid. Vol. I, p. 19.
39. Ibid. Vol. I, p. 22.
40. Ibid.
41. Ibid. Vol. I, p. 89.
42. Ibid. Vol. I, p. 90-91.
43. Ibid. Vol. I, pp. 90-91.
44. Ibid. Vol. I, p. 6.
45. Ibid. Vol. I, p. 3.
46. Ibid. Vol. I, p. 6.
47. David Perkins, *Calculus and its Origins*. Washington, DC: Mathematical Association of America, 2012, p. 19.
48. Victor J. Katz, "Ideas of Calculus in Islam and India," *Mathematics Magazine,* June 1995, pp. 163-174.
49. Victor J. Katz, "Ideas of Calculus in Islam and India," *Mathematics Magazine,* June 1995, pp. 163-174.
50. J.J. O'Connor and E.F. Robertson, "Abu Ali al-Hasan ibn al-Haytham," Mac Tutor, November 1999. https://mathshistory.st-andrews.ac.uk/Biographies/Al-Haytham.
51. Nuh Aydin, interview with the author, February 14, 2021.Ibid. Vol. I, p. 6.

CHAPTER SIX: Return to Basra

52. Ibid. Vol. I, p. 6.

53. Ibid. Vol. II, pp. xx-xxi.

54. Quoted in Abdul Ghafur Chaudhri, p. 112.

55. Ibid

56. Quoted in Ibn al-Haytham, *The Optics of Ibn al-Haytham*, tr. A.I. Sabra. London: The Warburg Institute, 1989, vol. II, p. lii.

57. Ibid. Vol. II, p. li.

58. Ibn al-Haytham, *On the Configuration of the World*, tr. Y. Tzvi Langermann. New York: Garland Publishing, Inc., 1990, p. 53.

59. Ibid. p. 8.

60. Quoted in Introduction, *On the Configuration of the World*, tr. Y. Tzvi Langermann. New York: Garland Publishing, Inc., 1990, pp. 9-10.

61. Quoted in Edward Rosen, *Copernicus and the Scientific Revolution*. Malabar, FL: Krieger, 1984, p. 174.

62. Quoted in Abdul Ghafur Chaudhri, p. 123.

CHAPTER SEVEN: "The Physicist"

63. Quoted in Ibn al-Haytham, 1989, vol. II, p. xxiv.

64. Quoted in A.I. Sabra, *Optics, Astronomy and Logic: Studies in Arabic Science and Philosophy*. Brookfield, Vermont: Variorum, 1994, p. 240.

65. Ibid. p. 239.

66. Quoted in Abdelhamid I. Sabra, "Problems of Scientific Borrowing: The Historical Background," *Science and Technology in the Eastern Arab Countries*. Princeton, NJ: Haskins Press, 1965, p. 11.

67. The Qur'an, The Family of Imran, Verse 136.

68. Quoted in "Ahl al-Kitab," Encyclopædia Britannica. Retrieved January 14, 2006, from Encyclopædia Britannica Premium Service, http://www.britannica.com/eb/article-9004124.

69. Quoted in J J O'Connor and E F Robertson, "Roger Bacon," University of St. Andrews, Scotland, website: http://www-history.mcs.st-andrews.ac.uk/Biographies/Bacon.html.

70 Constance Lowenthal, "Ghiberti, Lorenzo," Encyclopædia Britannica (2006). Retrieved January 23, 2006, from Encyclopædia Britannica Premium Service, http://www.britannica.com/eb/article-9036695

71 Quoted in "Was It Done with Mirrors?" 60 Minutes, August 3, 2003. CBS News website, http://www.cbsnews.com/stories/2003/01/16/60minutes/main536814.shtml.

72 Quoted in Bradley Steffens, Photography. San Diego: Lucent Books, 1991, p. 15.

73 Quoted in "Was It Done with Mirrors?" 60 Minutes, August 3, 2003. CBS News website, http://www.cbsnews.com/stories/2003/01/16/60minutes/main536814.shtml.

74 Quoted in "Was It Done with Mirrors?" 60 Minutes, August 3, 2003. CBS News website, http://www.cbsnews.com/sto-ries/2003/01/16/60minutes/main536814.shtml.

75 Francesca Fiorani, *The Shadow Drawing*. New York: Farrar, Straus and Giroux, 2020, p. 3.

76 Ibid. p. 11.

77 Ibid

78 Ibid.

79 Ibid. p. 16.

80 Quoted in Abdelhamid I. Sabra, "Problems of Scientific Borrowing: The Historical Background," *Science and Technology in the Eastern Arab Countries*. Princeton, NJ: Haskins Press, 1965, p. 3.

81 Quoted in "Ibn Al-Haytham to be a focus of the International Year of Light through partnering with 1001 Inventions," International Year of Light and Light-based Technologies. http://www.light2015.org/Home/About/Latest-News/November2014/Ibn-Al-Haytham-to-be-the-focus-of-the-International-Year-of-Light-through-partnering-with-1001-Inventions-.html.

82 Quoted in "Ibn Al-Haytham to be a focus of the International Year of Light through partnering with 1001 Inventions," International Year of Light and Light-based Technologies. http://www.light2015.org/Home/About/Latest-News/November2014/Ibn-Al-Haytham-to-be-the-focus-of-the-International-Year-of-Light-through-partnering-with-1001-Inventions-.html.

83 Quoted in Abdelhamid I. Sabra, "Ibn al-Haytham, Brief life of an Arab mathematician: died circa 1040," *Harvard Magazine*, September-October 2003. https://harvardmagazine.com/2003/09/ibn-al-haytham-html.

BIBLIOGRAPHY

Fiorani, Francesca, *The Shadow Drawing*. New York: Farrar, Straus and Giroux, 2020.

Haytham, Ibn al-, tr. Y. Tzvi Langermann. *On the Configuration of the World*. New York: Garland Publishing, 1990.

Haytham, Ibn al-, tr. A.I. Sabra. *The Optics of Ibn al-Haytham*. London: The Warburg Institute, 1989.

Hogendijk, J.P. *Ibn al-Haytham's* Completion of the Conics. New York: Springer-Verlag, 1985.

Lindberg, David C. *Studies in the History of Medieval Optics*. London: Variorum Reprints, 1983.

Omar, Saleh Beshara. *Ibn al-Hyatham's* Optics. Minneapolis: Bibliotheca Islamica, 1977.

Sabra, Abdelhamid I. and Jan P. Hogendijk, eds. *The Enterprise of Science in Islam: New Perspectives*. Cambridge, Massachusetts: MIT Press, 2003.

Sabra, A.I. *Theories of Light: from Descartes to Newton*. London: Oldbourne, 1967.

Sabra, A.I. *Optics, Astronomy and Logic: Studies in Arabic Science and Philosophy*. Brookfield, Vermont: Variorum, 1994.

Said, Hakim Mohammed, ed. *Ibn al-Haitham, Proceedings of the Celebrations of 1000th Anniversary*. Sadar, Pakistan: The Times Press, 1969.

A. Mark Smith. *Alhacen's Theory of Visual Perception*. Philadelphia: American Philosophical Society, 2001.

WEBSITES

Abdelhamid I. Sabra, "Ibn al-Haytham," Harvard Magazine, September-October 2003. An overview of the Islamic scholar's life and place in history by Abdelhamid I. Sabra, a translator of *The Book of Optics* and professor emeritus at Harvard University. https://www.harvardmagazine.com/2003/09/ibn-al-haytham-html.

"Ibn al-Haytham," Muslim Heritage. This page links to several articles about Ibn al-Haytham and his contributions to science. http://muslimheritage.com/keywords/ibn-al-haytham.

"Islam: Empire of Faith," PBS. An accompaniment to the PBS film, *Islam: Empire of Faith*, this website features timelines and articles on Islamic faith, culture, innovations, and historical figures. http://www.pbs.org/empires/islam/index.html.

"Who Was Ibn al-Haytham?" 1001 Inventions. Features a short biography of Ibn al-Haytham with links to articles by various scholars regarding the Abbasid scholar. http://www.ibnalhaytham.com/discover/who-was-ibn-al-haytham.

INDEX